The AI Matrix

Comparative Political Economy
Series Editor: Erik Jones

This series explores contemporary issues in comparative political economy. Pluralistic in approach, the books offer original, theoretically informed analyses of the interaction between politics and economics, and explore the implications for policy at the regional, national and supranational levels.

Published

The AI Matrix
Daniel Mügge, Regine Paul and Vali Stan

Central Bank Independence and the Future of the Euro
Panicos Demetriades

Europe and Northern Ireland's Future
Mary C. Murphy

The Magic Money Tree and Other Economic Tales
Lorenzo Forni

A Modern Migration Theory
Peo Hansen

The New Politics of Trade
Alasdair R. Young

The Political Economy of Housing Financialization
Gregory W. Fuller

Populocracy
Catherine Fieschi

Resilient Welfare States in the European Union
Anton Hemerijck and Robin Huguenot-Noël

The Rise of State Capital
Milan Babić

Whatever It Takes
George Papaconstantinou

The AI Matrix

Profits, Power, Politics

Daniel Mügge, Regine Paul and Vali Stan

agenda
publishing

First published in 2026 by Agenda Publishing

Agenda Publishing Limited
PO Box 185
Newcastle upon Tyne
NE20 2DH
www.agendapub.com

ISBN 978-1-78821-859-7

British Library Cataloguing-in-Publication Data
A catalogue record for this book is available from the British Library

Typeset by Newgen Publishing UK
Printed and bound in the UK by 4edge

EU GPSR authorized representative:
Logos Europe, 9 rue Nicolas Poussin, 17000 La Rochelle, France
contact@logoseurope.eu

Contents

Abbreviations   vii

Acknowledgements   ix

1   Beyond the hype: a global political economy view of AI   1

2   AI's deep roots and many forms   17

3   American AI and the Chinese challenge   35

4   Uneven effects across and within sectors   55

5   Uneven effects on labour   73

6   Uneven effects in the rest of the world   95

7   AI futures reconsidered   113

Notes   129

Index   145

Abbreviations

AI	artificial intelligence
AIT	artificial intelligence technology
AWS	Amazon Web Services
DARPA	Defense Advanced Research Project Agency
EU	European Union
FRT	facial recognition technology
FTC	Federal Trade Commission
GDP	gross domestic product
GDPR	General Data Protection Regulation
ICT	information and communications technology
IT	information technology
LLM	large language model
M&A	merger and acquisition
OECD	Organisation for Economic Co-operation and Development
UAE	United Arab Emirates
UK	United Kingdom
US	United States
WEF	World Economic Forum

Acknowledgements

Sharing an ardent sense of discontent with contemporary discussions of how AI transforms the entire economy (it cannot be that straightforward, can it now?), Daniel and Regine started this project in 2023 in a University of Amsterdam attic. The resulting sketch of a paper received helpful feedback from several colleagues, friends and conference attendees, most notably at the Deutsche Vereinigung für Politikwissenschaft (German Political Science Association) conference on political economy in Witten/Herdecke (September 2023) and the European Consortium for Political Research Joint Sessions in Lüneburg (March 2024). The boldest among them encouraged us to turn an excessively long theoretical paper into the introduction for a monograph that could reach a wider audience than the usual political economist gathering. Animated and intimidated, we agreed that an accessible book that would pull together the key conceptual tenets of critical political economy and economic geography with systematic illustrations of AI-related transformations across industries, labour markets and countries was, indeed, exactly the thing to do.

Adding brain space and a clear analytical gaze for economic indicators (and their limitations) in the fast-moving digital economy, Vali joined the team as co-author. And with Erik Jones and Alison Howson at Agenda Publishing we found a series editor and publisher convinced that the world needs a book like ours. We thank both for embracing our project enthusiastically from the start and for their support and editorial guidance throughout.

We thank Clarote for handmade cover art that captured so beautifully what we're on about. We came across her work on betterimagesof.ai: a hub for illustrations of the social and political sides of AI beyond stereotypical circuit boards or humanoid robots. Collaborating with Clarote has been a true joy.

We acknowledge generous funding from the University of Bergen Library for Open Access publication; and remain both grateful for and critically aware of our privilege in pulling this book to the front of a paywall. Daniel's and Vali's time invested in this book has been financed by the Nederlandse Organisatie voor Wetenschappelijk Onderzoek (Dutch Science Council) Vici project RegulAite (grant VI.C.211.32).

We experienced the research and writing process for this book as an intellectually stimulating journey. We remain grateful to each other for a truly collegial spirit, collective sparks of creativity and – yes, also – the many enjoyable chats over coffee and food in Amsterdam, Bucharest and Köln. Our thanks extend to Kath John Nordbø at the University of Bergen for assistance in digging out and collating long Excel tables of non-Western cases of AI-related labour movements, model developers and AI system providers.

1

Beyond the hype: a global political economy view of AI

I am here to bring the good news: AI will not destroy the world, and in fact may save it. [...] Productivity growth throughout the economy will accelerate dramatically, driving economic growth, creation of new industries, creation of new jobs, and wage growth, and resulting in a new era of heightened material prosperity across the planet.

Marc Andreessen, venture capitalist, 2023[1]

[A]n oligarchy is taking shape in America of extreme wealth, power, and influence that literally threatens our entire democracy, our basic rights and freedoms, and a fair shot for everyone to get ahead. [...] I'm equally concerned about the potential rise of a tech-industrial complex that could pose real dangers for our country as well.

Joe Biden, President of the United States, 15 January 2025[2]

How will artificial intelligence (AI) change economic life as we know it? We are not the first to ask this question, and we will not be the last. As the two epigraphs suggest, the answers can differ enormously. They range from hyper-optimistic prospects of AI revolutionizing, even saving, our economies and societies to doom-laden fears of wealth and power concentration among tech billionaires, with disastrous consequences for everyone else. As political economists, we have found ourselves increasingly disturbed by the narrowness and spectacle of this debate. Where are public interventions and institutions as shapers of AI? What role do the hyped AI narratives themselves play as agents of change? How does today's geoeconomic context affect AI development? And where does this leave the roughly 6 billion people who live outside China and the Global North? These questions are central to current developments, but public debates routinely ignore them. So, when we ask how AI will change economic life as we know it, our answer – this book – offers the political economy perspective of the "AI matrix": a complex but patterned set of tech-related transformations shaped by corporate profit-seeking, hyped tech narratives and competitive politics. Using this wider lens, we hope to do more justice to the complexity of AI's transformative features and get a stronger analytical grip on what is unfolding around us.

The techno-solutionists and optimists imbue AI with messianic qualities. Like Andreessen, some extol AI's ability to "save the world". Many of the most sanguine stories come from AI developers or financiers themselves. But sundry researchers, too, portray AI as a hero: it prevents climate collapse, promotes sustainable development and fights famines through revolutionized agriculture. And should escape from Earth be our only survival option after all, AI can at least tell us how to procure oxygen on Mars.

At a widely broadcast gig from the 2024 World Economic Forum (WEF) in Davos, Black Eyed Peas frontman will.i.am celebrated AI as the great equalizer; a power to end poverty. And he is not the only one to hope that AI brings unparalleled prosperity. Microsoft's chief technology officer Kevin Scott announced nothing short of a "reprogramming" of the American Dream, with AI generating growth for all, regardless of job automation.[3] Consultancies claim that firms already harness some of this potential. In their 2024 "State of AI" report, McKinsey consultants suggest that AI-powered tools have empowered many firms to cut costs and generate new revenue. PwC predicts AI's worldwide contribution to reach $15.7 trillion by 2030; another McKinsey report expects generative AI alone to generate $4.4 trillion.[4]

Such rhetoric should not be swallowed uncritically, not least because consultancies themselves sell precious advisory services on the back of the hype they nurture. But governments and companies do take it seriously, and if nothing else, it informs the decisions they make about AI. The Commission of the European Union, for example, expects AI to bring "increasing productivity across all economic sectors", "tremendous opportunities for Europe's economic growth", and an "increased economic dynamism", which will "create new employment opportunities and outweigh the potential job losses".[5] Comparable expectations about productivity, growth and job boosts thrive, among others, in Brazil, China, India, the United Arab Emirates (UAE), the United Kingdom (UK) and the United States (US). Faced with such predictions, the question no longer seems to be whether one should use AI, but rather where exactly it can deliver a competitive advantage. A search in global library catalogues for "artificial intelligence" and "economy" reveals that guidance on *how to optimize* organizations with AI is booming just as much as the tech itself.

Switching to the pessimistic view, historian Yuval Noah Harari has castigated generative AI systems like ChatGPT as an "alien invasion" bound to terminate human-dominated history.[6] His voice joins a larger doomsday choir. Toby Ord heralds our arrival at a "precipice", the point at which we have invented the technological means to annihilate ourselves, and fellow AI commentators Nick Bostrom and Yoshua Bengio – controversial in their own right – seem to agree.[7] Others worry less about humanity's extinction but more about the damage AI does here and now: to democratic elections, to information access, to copyright and creative production, to the rule of law, to social equality and to individual freedom. Training data and models reinforce societal biases against those already marginalized, including ethnic minorities. These critics see harmful AI rooted in the exclusionary and undemocratic ideologies that feed tech development, such as white supremacy, misogyny, or anti-poor sentiment.[8] Mass surveillance and algorithmic processing of behavioural data for exploitation and repression could push us toward authoritarian market societies.[9]

Here too, economic dynamics loom large. Doomsayers fear that material gains in one place will systematically translate into losses in another. The main threat is "A.I.-supercharged corporations destroying the environment and the working class in their pursuit of shareholder value".[10] In *Weapons of Math Destruction*, Cathy O'Neil has lamented the harms and injustices inflicted by algorithmic systems – in failed credit-worthiness checks, denial of welfare benefits, unsuccessful job applications, or life-changing prison sentences – which only count as "collateral damage" to companies bent on earning money with such systems.[11]

Already vulnerable populations are especially exposed. In an unsavoury amalgamation of austerity, punitive welfare practices, datafication of welfare states, and racialized and gendered algorithmic biases, AI helps to cut state expenditures by penalizing people whose identities (for example, as a poor, non-white caregiver) already relegate them to the socio-economic margins.[12] In this view, AI is little more than a rehash of old modes of exploitation. James Bridle sees AI as an ally of "an out-of-control economic system that immiserates many and continues to widen the gap between rich and poor".[13] To many on the pessimistic side, AI development serves capital owners as the latest form of exclusive wealth extraction rather than creating more prosperous and equitable societies.

Sceptics also foresee a mounting redundancy of human-performed labour – if not a potential threat to human life itself – posed by autonomous hyperintelligent machines reminiscent of *A Space Odyssey*'s HAL 9000. During a 2024 Paris tech conference, Elon Musk mused that as jobs would become "optional" and "kind of like a hobby", a humanity that no longer needs to provide goods and services for itself would lose a key source of fulfilment.[14] This is not just alarmist talk from a controversial "tech bro". Reputable economists also gesture at "a world without work" as reflected in the title of one of Daniel Susskind's books, albeit in less polemic terms. Similarly, the WEF forecasts a loss of roughly "14 million jobs, or 2% of current employment" worldwide.[15] And even if AI does not replace workers, it may render them more exploitable rather than augmenting their capabilities by squeezing maximal productivity gains and performance out of each worker. Such bleak scenarios depict a power concentration at the expense of ordinary citizens, workers and especially vulnerable populations, who become dependent and dispensable.[16] Here, AI does not enlarge the economic pie to the benefit of many; instead, it redistributes wealth from the many to the few.[17]

In this book, we concentrate on the economic side of AI, broadly conceived. AI reverberates throughout our societies and politics in worrying ways that go far beyond the economic domain. But as political economists, we recognize that present-day AI development is, in the first instance, a money game. AI development and diffusion is driven by some of the largest companies in the world. Annual investment in the technology goes into hundreds of billions of dollars. The *effects* of AI as it evolves resonate broadly. The *drivers* of what goes on, however, are largely found in corporate rationales and decisions, whether in C-suite deliberations at Microsoft's headquarters about where to build new data centres, or in the ruminations of the small enterprise next door about whether investing in AI will be worth it.

The current debate about the economic dimension of AI (both its effects and its drivers) is crucial but also, we argue, misguided. More often than not, it is too narrowly technological and economistic. It thrives on unduly bombastic and universalizing claims about AI as a force in human history. The debate routinely ignores four central insights of political economy that go a long way to adding nuance and depth. The typically grandiose pronouncements about how AI will or will not transform the world downplay the role of the political agency of states and other actors in shaping technological innovation and its effects. They obscure the powerful role of narratives and tech imaginaries in encouraging or obstructing regulatory, fiscal or other government action. They nourish and are themselves fed by an intensifying geopolitical "AI race" among a few global superpowers and the super-rich tech business elites, with little to no consideration for the wellbeing of most people on this planet. And they are inattentive to the effects of highly uneven AI transformations within and between sectors, workplaces or countries worldwide. These four blind spots of much contemporary debate guide us as we explore the global political economy of AI: as a matrix shaped by profit-seeking, hyped narratives and competitive politics in a geoeconomic context.

The role of political agency and institutions in AI transformations

Technological innovation does not just emerge spontaneously out of genius brains and research labs. Instead, it is deeply shaped by political agency and institutions. Taking inspiration from science and technology studies, we appreciate how AI research, development and its uses are socially embedded in wider economic contexts and government strategies.[18] Those include regulatory and legal frameworks, the political tussle about them, institutions such as social safety nets and democratic checks and balances, but also public investment programmes. Hype around lab-based AI innovation might suggest otherwise, but it continues a much older history of the development and diffusion of large-scale tech systems backed by states and political action.

Consider the wave of tech deregulation and the investment boost after Donald Trump re-entered the White House in 2025. Much critique of AI and other digital technologies is not about the tech itself but about how it is made, used, diffused and regulated. That includes monopoly business models, mass value extraction from private data without profit-sharing, regulatory arbitrage or legal mobilizations that enable the enclosure (or colonization) of publicly available data for machine learning models as corporate property.[19]

At its most abstract, we have to appreciate that AI evolves in the shadow of capitalism rather than in an alternative socio-economic order. In capitalism, AI development is essentially profit driven. Normative discussions over whether this is a good thing aside, this profit orientation unambiguously shapes tech development and governance. Alternative visions of a tech future would involve collective action from workers, tighter regulation, and wider societal discussion over how Big Tech's massive profits should be distributed. Proposals include different taxation models for tech-related capital, or an automation fund paid by firms to co-finance a universal basic income for workers facing automation risk.

Highly visible and influential people try to steer AI through government policies or protest. On the side supporting a techno-optimist vision, figures like Elon Musk have propagated and implemented public sector "cost-saving drives", frequently coupled with AI rollouts. On the critical side, consider activist Cory Doctorow, who diligently curates evidence about the political economy of Big Tech, and tech journalist Brian Merchant whose *Blood in the Machine* blog reports on the American state-economy-AI complex. Or a whistleblower such as AI ethicist Timnit Gebru, whom Google sacked for revealing racial biases in the company's models. She publicly lamented AI's enormous carbon footprint and questioned the wonders of large language models (LLMs) in the famous *Stochastic Parrots* paper, co-authored with Emily Bender and others.[20]

Whistleblowers have a key role to mend the governance shortcomings associated with digital tech. Without insiders such as Gebru, the public would know much less about Big Tech's dark sides, be they toxic work cultures, environmental damages or the promotion of harmful AI models. Such revelations can mobilize others as in the 20,000-strong Google walkout, strengthen existing AI-critical social movements, or spur the establishment of activist research centres like the AI Now Institute. Just how much power such individuals can have in the political economy at large remains an open question. But they frequently do succeed in getting their message heard.

Still, much of the actual steering of tech development's impact is done by and through states, whether intentionally or not. With his take on market sociology, Karl Polanyi underlined how governments manage socio-economic relations through their political interventions. And comparative political economists have shown time and again how differently countries organize and govern their economies, including the development, application and diffusion of technologies. As we argue throughout this book, this is true for AI as well. From investment schemes and intellectual property rights to sectoral first-mover advantages and labour automation, how AI markets develop and affect our societies depends on whether these markets are left to the relentless forces of unbridled capitalism, or whether regulation counteracts monopoly formation, the crowding out of the human factor in labour markets, or offloading environmental damage onto citizens, especially those in the Global South.

We do not subscribe to a facile political voluntarism, however. How AI plays out is conditioned by how actors navigate the structural constraints they confront. First and foremost, governments need to collect taxes or generate income from wealth funds, should they have them, to cover AI-related expenses. Societal divisions often limit the appetite for cross-class solidarity. In an open global economy, governments face systematic incentives to promote national industry champions. And whereas these factors vary across countries – an important reason to embrace nuance – they do shape how AI comes to transform the global political economy. Appreciating political agency amidst these structural constraints, we need to look beyond techno-determinist and universalist accounts to understand real-world AI transformations.

Grand AI narratives typically ignore how institutional choices shape the technology's trajectory and impact. Who wins or loses from innovation also depends on the institutional context in which it is applied. As in earlier waves of automation, conflicting interests raise distributive questions: how are the spoils shared when worker productivity goes up? Public authorities' market interventions have typically put "consumer welfare" at the heart of their activities, checking whether corporate concentration raised product prices. Much of the digital economy got a green light. After all, many services (think social media, search engines, and so on) are nominally free to consumers. Recently, the mood has shifted. Regulators in institutions such as the Federal Trade Commission (FTC) have reemphasized other socio-political implications, including worker welfare and corporate power abuses beyond straightforward rent-seeking. How states could and should intervene in the tech sector remains itself hotly debated, including among economists and other academics.

Government interventions or strong unions can shelter sectors and their workers from innovation-fuelled competition, force companies to share technologies or redistribute the wealth generated through them. Daron Acemoglu and Simon Johnson have suggested that worker mobilization against deleterious AI impacts could make the difference between a dystopian economic future and a more hopeful, equitable and affluent one.[21] We agree. Carefully managed automation could usher in the long-desired emancipation from Marxian estrangement through repetitive, dirty and strenuous labour. If the gains from AI accrue mainly to the owners of capital, however, inequality will rise further without making many workers better off.[22]

To chart different approaches to governing tech development more systematically, comparative political economists have explored varieties of platformization and tech regulation. They highlight the impact of labour relations, welfare states and financial markets on AI transformations. Robert Boyer, for example, distinguishes three stylized models of platform economies. The US, he argues, explores a "liberal commodification" path with lean regulation and oligopolistic power concentration in Silicon Valley. China pursues "a society of control" in which data and behavioural predictions help ensure social control over citizens. The European Union (EU), finally, leans towards a "new Common" model, emphasizing citizen interests and democratic control.[23] While potentially starry-eyed about the EU's noble motives in an intensifying AI race, such analyses usefully show that digitalization is not one universal, uniform process but that it balances power relations between states, markets and citizens in different ways. K. Sabeel Rahman and Kathleen Thelen have dissected political choices further. The US has offered a "permissive" political landscape for large-scale platformization, owing to fragmented regulatory capacities, weak stakeholders, the pro-consumer orientation of antitrust law, and the thorough financialization of the economy. Europe, in contrast, features stronger organized interests, social justice concerns, powerful regulators, and long-term industrial policy and relations, all leading to tighter constraints for platform companies as exemplified by General Data Protection Regulation (GDPR) as well as the more recent Digital Markets Act, the Digital Services Acts, and the AI Act.[24]

Taken together, such work highlights the institutional embeddedness of tech dynamics and how they reverberate throughout economies. At the same time, in its eagerness to draw out ideal types and differences, it also papers over dynamics that AI trajectories around the world have in common. For that reason, our own analyses below explore differences across the globe and across sectors from the bottom up, starting from the historical and empirical differences and interlinkages we find in the wild.

The power of distorted tech narratives

Our second source of scepticism towards grand AI narratives is constructivist social science. When governments, businesses, investors or activists form opinions, they do not just draw on robust evidence. Inevitably, AI debates are dominated by speculative narratives and bold extrapolations of current trends. That also holds for future-oriented economic analyses about AI's impact on productivity, national competitiveness, labour markets, welfare, national sovereignty and so on. Expectations (at least by the more powerful among us) considerably shape the direction of the AI transformation. In the language of science and technology studies, AI narratives themselves play a performative role. Their inbuilt expectations funnel funding, reorder research and development priorities, lead to large-scale public procurement, trigger investment in startups, skew hiring and firing decisions, provoke regulatory choices, and shape foreign and trade policies. When the Chinese company DeepSeek released its cheap but powerful model in January 2025, bullish expectations about the market for AI computer hardware evaporated, and Nvidia stocks lost almost a fifth of their value – hundreds of billions of dollars in market capitalization.

The performative power of AI narratives unfolds in several ways. To begin with, generative AI (the likes of ChatGPT) absorbs almost all attention. Very different forms of AI – like those used in robotics or facial recognition technology (FRT), for example – hardly feature in discussions about how "AI" shapes the economy. In fact, very diverse technologies fall under the AI-heading, and they have different technological needs, require different kinds of data and amounts of money to build, and spawn different market and power dynamics. A public discussion that unwittingly concentrates on the flashy and showstopping AI inevitably misconstrues the diverse impact that these technologies have, a point to which we return time and again throughout this book.

Moreover, AI has been deeply shaped by Silicon Valley ideology. Key ingredients include an uncritical techno-solutionism whereby social problems can be fixed with a new app or model, a sense of moral superiority by which the smart tech developers know what is best for everyone else, a deep distrust of government activity, but also an anti-human mindset where moneymaking and technological progress can legitimize human suffering.[25]

This mix of ideas has morphed into a dubious groupthink blind to tech's detrimental impact on human wellbeing and the planet's health.[26] Mark Zuckerberg's communicative nucleus is exemplary: he presents Facebook as a platform where smart people thrive to make the world a better place, a profit-making company masquerading as a social entrepreneur.[27] Moral claims are conflated with the more or less open pursuit of hard-nosed economic interests. At the fringe end, a handful of tech billionaires plan an escape from planet Earth, seen as teetering on the brink of destruction and popular mass revolt – ironically fuelled by the same tech universe that enriches the Bezoses, Musks, and Zuckerbergs of this world.[28] This thinking reached its apogee when in 2025, President Trump mandated Elon Musk – a tech billionaire who had greatly benefitted from government contracts and funds – to hollow out the federal administration following a techno-solutionist austerity paradigm.

Few businesses and governments fully buy into this ideology. Still, its promise and energy resonate widely. Echoes of techno-optimism inform corporate and policy narratives. Grand stories unambiguously extolling AI as "the future" not only serve the interests of AI salespeople and investors. They allow any firm adopting AI to signal "future readiness" to its clients and shareholders. Consultancies like BCG, McKinsey, Accenture and PwC hail AI as "a new factor of production", offering pricey consultancy hours to CEOs who are anxious not to miss the AI boat.[29] This is where AI narratives hit the ground running: "hypes gain their real performative momentum by pointing to vast opportunities that lie ahead" and to benefits foregone if one does not act immediately.[30] Billions and billions of investment and policy priorities hang on loose hopes and promises.

How about governments, then? How do ideas and expectations about AI's economic impact shape their policies? Here we draw on cultural political economy, according to which "economic imaginaries" help stabilize hegemonic economic orders under pressure.[31] The need to address legitimacy deficits is a long-standing theme in this line of analysis. Inspired by Marxian views of crises and periodic breakdowns as inherent features of capitalism, thinkers like Claus Offe or Jürgen Habermas explored how states react to them. Offe saw the constant tension between economic dynamism and the need to mend social ills and inequality as a source of welfare states' persisting legitimacy crisis. Habermas, too, illustrated how states' contradictory roles and actions trigger severe legitimacy crises as they attempt to balance capital accumulation, social welfare and democratic legitimacy.

For a small number of countries, the growth of global AI markets lets sovereign funds fill their welfare pockets thanks to rising tech stocks. Norway's large *oljefond* is an outstanding example, investing in Alphabet, Meta and other US tech firms and wielding record profits of $222 billion (or 13 per cent of its total value) in 2024. But the country's oil- and gas-based rentier economy is an outlier, and fantasies of tech-generated wealth for the state purse remain out of reach for most others. That said, for most governments the legitimizing potential of AI hangs not on tangible tax income or higher returns on public investment, but on vague promises of brighter socio-economic futures, regardless of whether they materialize or not.[32] Even as frustration and disillusionment among citizens rise, the prospect of a happy socio-economic ending is dangled in front of them. If this optimistic AI narrative sticks, politicians are momentarily off the hook.

Most reflections so far have focused on (more or less) liberal, democratic and capitalist societies. As it turns out, elites in authoritarian regimes with different blends of capitalism – say Middle Eastern rentier economies or state capitalism in China – are no less likely to promise technological progress as a magic key to economic prosperity and social progress to legitimize their rule. The Chinese administration justifies its efforts in the AI field by "socioeconomic development and the progress of human civilization", whereas Saudi Arabia wants to mitigate the impending end of the profitable fossil energy age by turning to AI as the next source of income and power.[33]

This future-oriented temporality of AI-related state action unites jurisdictions beyond regime differences. The public framing of AI as an engine for socio-economic prosperity answers to governments' need to find the next big idea to cling to when political legitimacy crumbles. Those in political office – whether elected or not – may well sustain AI-optimistic discourses simply because without them, an entire socio-economic model or political regime might be on the line. The AI hype then matters in more material ways, because it allows governments to ignore warnings and push AI development forwards instead. It marginalizes alternative paths to AI, those not dominated by quick profit maximization but by what societies want and need from these technologies. AI's impact thus extends beyond its mere technological presence and actions; it captivates the imagination, for better or worse. A big part of its effect lies in the reactions it provokes, as people anticipate its arrival and the changes it brings.

None of this means that AI is just a fad without any substance or potential for change; far from it. What it does mean, however, is that the stories and imaginaries about AI that circulate have as much "economic impact" as the material applications of the technologies themselves. By connecting visions of AI-related prosperity and competitiveness to material decisions on the political-economic ground, the hopeful portrayals of the tech transformations that seem within reach may well become more realistic. Like self-fulfilling prophecies, narratives about emergent tech can "talk AI into being" as they motivate funding, procurement decisions, regulation or enforcement actions.[34]

The self-fulfilling prophecy of a geoeconomic "race to AI"

One future scenario has become particularly powerful: the global AI race. Days after resuming office, President Trump announced a $500 billion investment into AI infrastructure under a new public-private consortium called Stargate (to be fair, most of the money would come from private investors). The haste went along with a widely propagated "there-is-no-alternative" logic: if the US does not invest massively in infrastructure, computing capacity and data centres to lead AI tech development, China certainly will – somewhat ironically, given that just days later, the DeepSeek breakthrough indicated how tech leadership may also emerge from more judicious use of scarce resources.

Part of this catching-up imperative responds to wider geoeconomic dynamics: in large companies' global struggle over infrastructural power and market shares, states and regional blocs move away from open economies and define their role as more selective facilitators of whatever seems to be safeguarding their sovereignty and economic prosperity best.[35] Following an assessment by the European Parliament, the EU's AI Act came with hopes that a clear regulatory environment in the large common market could generate €294.9 billion in additional GDP and 4.6 million additional jobs by 2030.[36] This would, so the promise, boost investment in and deployment of AI products in Europe and create a market with new revenues, jobs and European tech leadership.[37] If there was any doubt, the EU-commissioned Draghi report put it to rest, clarifying Brussels' geopolitical ambitions within these competitiveness claims.[38] Promoting the AI sector has become crucial in the continent's quest for "strategic autonomy".[39]

Jurisdictions worldwide tell strikingly similar stories of geoeconomic dynamics and geopolitical struggles over AI leadership. "We" must advance "our" national economy's position in a fierce "race to AI" by all means, simply because we otherwise risk not only foregoing the socio-economic benefits of innovation but also losing the ability to act autonomously from Big Tech and political adversaries. Already under President Biden both the National Artificial Intelligence Initiative Act and a report by the US National Security Commission on AI diagnosed an existential need for continued AI leadership.[40] As the latter suggests in an online summary of its 2021 report: "China is a competitor possessing the might, talent, and ambition to challenge America's technological leadership, military superiority, and its broader position in the world".

On the other side of the struggle, in a recent strategy on global AI governance President Xi Jinping articulates China's opposition to the diffusion of Western AI systems and regulations as a matter of stopping those powers from "intervening in other countries' internal affairs, social systems and social order, as well as jeopardizing the sovereignty of other states".[41] We will explore later how China exploits this narrative when spreading its tech across the Global South, including facial recognition technology, where it is a global market leader.

The discursive marriage of economic competitiveness with the geopolitically-motivated drive for digital sovereignty moulds states' AI funding and regulation. To counter the threat of Chinese AI leadership, the federal US government heavily invests in research and development, and it promotes access to high-quality open data, workforce development, public-private partnerships and innovation-friendly regulation. On the other side of the Atlantic, Brussels has set in motion fiscal and regulatory interventions to buttress its own vision of digital sovereignty. That includes boosting public investment and research programmes for homegrown technology, but also the world's largest single market for "trustworthy" AI products, which putatively follow democratic norms and fundamental human rights.[42]

The European Commission's vision may come across as naïve when compared with massive US investment and Chinese LLM breakthroughs. And yet, Europe's political action on AI – lubricated by the ambition to find a competitive niche – creates a more rights-based alternative to the American innovation-first approach and China's focus on societal control.[43] Alarmed perceptions of other major players' positioning and strategic moves fuse with hyped expectations about the potential fruits of AI leadership. These discourses create a sense of urgency and encourage political action, leaving little space for public debate about the distribution of AI-related benefits, costs and harms within societies and across the globe, or just how much AI is really needed, and where. In essence, geopolitical competition explains governments' willingness to push ahead with AI development even in the face of significant risks and dangers, and it shapes their eagerness to diffuse it abroad, not only as commercial bridge heads, but also as part of digital zones of influence.

The spatial unevenness of global AI transformations

The final blind spot in mainstream debates may be the biggest of them all: where is the rest of the world in discussions of AI transformation that rarely venture beyond the US–China–EU triangle? Three inspirations from economic geography shift our analytical gaze beyond a world seemingly populated only by a few Big Tech corporations, their leaders and even fewer national superpowers.

First, national economies and tech models are embedded in a global context that both enables and constrains them: where do countries stand in the global economic hierarchy (which typically is hard to change)? Do countries control resources which others need in order to develop or deploy technology? The position that countries and leading corporations attain in global hierarchies has always shaped where riches accumulate and how they are distributed. There is no reason why AI-driven growth and disparities should be any different to say fossil resources, car manufacturing or financial services. Cross-country comparisons, helpful as they are for showcasing capitalist diversity, overlook how variants of digital capitalism are interdependent and mutually constitutive as subtypes in a global capitalist order. Just as countries' position in global financial orders has shaped the terms on which they have access to financial resources, locally specific but globally connected political economies feature in tech development.

As Jamie Peck and Rachel Phillips observe, local platform economies may have specific features but always interact with the dominant US template of disruptive innovation: "The shape, evolution, and global footprint of platform capitalism cannot be dissociated from these geographical origins, even as the phenomenon is not reducible to the global diffusion of a Silicon Valley-style model".[44] With their close interactions between entrepreneurs and local universities (and backed by state and venture capital), tech clusters from Bangalore to Lagos, from Recife to Tel Aviv, and from Shenzhen to the iconic Silicon Valley have more in common than their position on a geographical or political map suggests.[45] At the same time, digital technologies further integrate value chains and accumulation steered from the Global North even as supply chains themselves may fragment further.[46]

This is no economically-determined process: AI transformations are not only driven by autonomous visions and actions of sovereign states, but also by the interactions between "digital empires" and their struggle over global influence.[47] Nation-centric comparisons tend to overlook such interdependencies. How does the fact that Africa holds only 0.2 per cent of the global computing infrastructure perpetuate power differentials that existed long before digital tech?[48] In Chapter 6, we explore how colonial legacies shape AI experiences in the majority world more closely.[49]

Second, broad-brush analyses of AI transformations obscure substantial intra-country disparities. Even to the degree that they are useful units of analysis, national economies are not transformed "as a whole". Instead, changes are fundamental in some (work-)places and sectors, whereas others remain relatively untouched. Workers in East Africa and South Asia may benefit from their regions having become global hubs for outsourced data labelling labour. And the click workers in Nairobi's Silicon Savannah will experience the AI transformation in a different way from their compatriots in rural areas without electricity. The same would be true of a non-unionized German Amazon warehouse worker under constant AI-powered surveillance, who may look jealously at the well-organized automotive industry worker whose collective agreement protects their job (even if that protection is not set in stone either).

AI-driven changes amplify but sometimes also cushion socio-economic inequalities and political grievances within countries. Either way, what happens heavily depends on the specific context. Workers in some sectors may have more in common with their peers abroad than with other workers in their own national economy. What is more, any discussion of Global South tech hubs as the hopeful carriers of income for local communities glosses over new forms of precarity and work-related harm, for example in AI "sweatshops" in the Philippines or Kenya in which workers produce clean, meticulously annotated data for shiny models, often under appalling conditions (more in Chapter 5).

Third, if we only concentrate on AI leaders, we fail to capture how the global AI diffusion matters for countries, firms and workers elsewhere in the world. According to a PwC study published before the LLM hype, a full 70 per cent of the global economic impact of AI tech advances will accumulate in China and the US (measured as GDP boosts of 21 and 14.5 per cent by 2030, respectively), with much of the remaining gains concentrated in Europe and the more economically developed parts of Asia.[50] Africa, Latin America and "other Asian markets" would see "modest increases" in GDP through AI adoption at best, according to these projections. What sounds like non-news, however, strikes us as important: such projections imply that most countries beyond the Global North will be left further behind, and that asymmetries and dependencies between them and the high-tech leaders will only increase. So much for a technological tide that lifts all boats.

Following Rachel Adams and other decolonial political economy scholars, we see contemporary forms of exploitation for and with AI as recent stitches in a much older tapestry: "those who are being exploited and oppressed in the production and use of AI are the very same people who have historically been exploited and oppressed by global powers: women, people of colour, and citizens of the majority world".[51] This spatial-temporal connection of AI transformation to other political economy phenomena raises additional questions: to what extent does AI production in global tech hubs rely on the exploitation of resources and labour elsewhere? How is the dominance of the US and China in AI related to, for example, Brazilian, Canadian or South African attempts to produce, use and regulate these technologies? And how do the political and economic priorities of governments in the majority world co-shape AI diffusion patterns?

As we will show, globe-spanning AI hierarchies do not mean that the impact of technologies across more peripheral economies and societies is even. The intensifying geopolitical tension between American and Chinese capitalism, industrial AI policy and digital imperial ambitions fashions complex interdependences. Any less influential government's attempt to regulate, finance or socially cushion AI development thus also hangs on its position in the Sino-American struggle. Overall, grand narratives about AI's transformative power and state-centric broad-brush comparisons hide the intricacies, stratifications and contradictions in how AI changes the global political economy.

We approach AI-generated transformations as instances of variegated political-economic configurations.[52] They differ across places, industries and societal groups. At the same time, these differences are not coincidental but systematically related to each other, just as different economic country profiles are rooted in, and reproduced by, global hierarchies. The analytical advantage of "spatializing" political economy research is that it can navigate between "grandiose theorization and pedantic description".[53] With this perspective, we can capture the uneven yet connected development of digital capitalism, namely, how partial experiences of tech transformation across the world, across labour markets and across sectors mutually constitute global politico-economic relations around AI technologies. Analysing articulations of AI in capitalism as variegated also adheres to a research-ethical principle of decolonial knowledge production.[54] If we avoid "theorizing from a presumptive center [and instead engage in] transversal-relational analysis" and disruption of orthodoxies, we are not only better equipped to unpack the "complex articulations and respective positionalities" in economic governance[55]; we may also increase awareness of the often-colonial politics of knowledge production on AI transformation in the singular.

With these analytical prisms, our book explores how AI technologies fit into the world as political economists understand it: one in which political and economic power blend into and condition each other. Critically reviewing the US-dominated history of AI development (Chapter 2), we carve out the constitutive role of security-oriented state institutions, public funding and optimization narratives for getting AI off the ground. In recent years, government priorities and rationales have continued to shape AI development (Chapter 3). With China's arrival on the AI scene, Sino-American rivalry has also infected AI policy. At the same time, the increasing financial opportunities AI seems to offer have attracted enormous public and private funding and inserted a much more directly commercial dynamic into tech development. We then demonstrate AI's uneven diffusion across economic sectors (Chapter 4) and labour markets (Chapter 5). Even as we concentrate only on the richer parts of the world in these chapters, we show how technology reinforces existing hierarchies rather than transforming the underlying logic of capitalist economies. Shifting the gaze beyond the epicentres of AI development (Chapter 6), we observe an imperative of catch-up races among a few richer countries. These races involve using different AI governance initiatives to build their own tech empires, whereas poorer countries tend to reinforce their structural dependencies on US- or China-led technology in pursuit of their own political and economic agendas. Our final discussion (Chapter 7) centres less profit-driven models for tech development and existing forms of resistance against exploitative innovation. We return to our political economy concern with AI, with a normative twist: whom does the technology benefit and what does it take to share the costs and benefits of innovation more equally?

2

AI's deep roots and many forms

AI is a notoriously blurry and ultimately misleading concept. Popular imagery suggests something faintly magical and ethereal about it. As a non-profit artist collaboration highlights on its webpage, "abstract, futuristic and science-fiction-inspired images of AI" not only "hinder understanding of the technology's already significant societal and environmental impact", but they also set "unrealistic expectations" about AI's capabilities and "mask the accountability of the humans" involved in producing and using this technology.[1] (This mission statement chimes with our scholarly approach to tech, and informed our search for the book's cover artwork.) How we imagine and talk about AI and its historical genesis shapes where we look for its transformative potential. It is essential to appreciate the biases in common AI histories – mostly written as hagiographies of tech innovators with little sensitivity to historical context – and the diversity of technologies that sail under the AI flag.

As a socio-technical construct, "AI" is deeply entrenched not only in economic value generation and productivity enhancement, but also in political expectations about how innovation can sustain public welfare, security and stability. When businesspeople or policymakers discuss AI, they rarely dissect technological specificities but offer blanket statements instead, presupposing, for example, that no one can afford to miss the "AI transformation", or that it will decide future wars. Narratives about what AI is and might do shape tech development, funding decisions, pilot cases and broader rollouts in ways that are frequently at odds with actual technological capabilities. Such discursive distortion obscures how diverse AI technologies' economic impact is. And it hides how these technologies emerge out of equally variable socio-economic contexts. Understanding "what AI is" and how our current imaginaries of AI came about requires more than enumerating the technologies that are "in scope".

The history of AI has been told many times. Excitement about successive shiny novelties infuses public debates while attention shifts from the Metaverse to generative AI to agentic AI as the next big thing. As an antidote, it is important to appreciate tech's ubiquitous mundane uses: payment and navigation systems, entertainment services and so many invisible systems that grease the wheels of contemporary societies. To gauge AI development away from the spotlights, we zoom in on aspects that stand out from a political economy angle, whether they are at the cutting edge of AI development or not. As a cluster of technologies, AI possesses something special and transformative in general. At the same time, "the political economy of AI" suggests a uniform, coherent set of technologies, when in reality, AI applications, systems and companies are enormously diverse, frustrating attempts to come up with definitive definitions. Different AI systems' technical affordances shape AI's political economy impacts beyond the institutional and geoeconomic factors we discuss later in the book.

The definitional challenge of AI

One approach to capturing AI is to define it as "automation of cognition".[2] While this broad definition can accommodate a large variety of technologies, purely pre-programmed algorithmic models fall out of its scope because they do not share the "cognition" criterion of the definition. These so-called symbolic approaches to AI have been part of the research field for decades but generate little excitement at present. What sets AI apart from other algorithms and generates hype and investment is that it can learn from data and feedback (both machine and human). Such machine learning, trained on large amounts of data, is the most prominent approach to AI.

Out in the wild, AI does not exist in isolation. Like any other software, AI needs hardware and other software to operate. In early 2025, insatiable hunger for computer chips powering AI propelled Nvidia from an obscure gaming equipment producer to one of the world's most valuable companies, with a market capitalization rivalling Apple and Microsoft. Without semiconductors, there is no AI. As we explore more fully in Chapter 3, a political economy of AI must therefore also consider components across the whole technology stack: computer chips, data storage, fibreoptic cables, cloud computing and so on. The exploitative conditions under which metals like cobalt – vital to batteries – are dug up in war-ravaged regions like the Congo belongs to the political economy of AI as much as OpenAI's business strategies.

But it does not end there. People build AI. Not just developers writing code, but thousands of people label and clean the data used to train algorithms, and hundreds of millions of internet users unwittingly create the digital content that feeds them, from YouTube videos to GitHub projects. AI flowers on a bed of hidden, and often underpaid, human labour. In 2016, AlphaGo beat champion Lee Sedol at Go, a game that dwarfs chess in complexity. DeepMind's programmers reportedly trained it on 30 million games, which people had generated in millions of hours of playing Go on their computers, and recoded players' strategies and results.[3] Little did the players know that they would train a competitor to beat them all. Moreover, many real-world applications combine AI with other technologies as crucial interfaces between AI-powered apps and people: more or less self-driving cars, cameras in public spaces, robots in a factory, drones, or smartphones and watches. There is no clear point at which AI begins or ends. It is mixed with other technologies and mundane human inputs, without which it cannot function.

Given that it is the interaction of these technologies that matters, it is often difficult to pinpoint the contribution AI has made to any specific dynamic, much like trying retroactively to extract eggs from pancake batter. AI is integral to the business models of platform companies like Uber, but it is just one ingredient among others, including data, technical infrastructure and human labour. Lest we get tied up in unhelpful definitional knots, we will try to clarify what we write about at any given point, but we also use the term AI with some liberty. To highlight the diversity of technologies under the AI heading, we at times also switch to "AI technologies", or AITs.[4]

So, what capabilities do AITs have? What can we do with them? First, they can identify and recognize patterns in large datasets. What makes people click specific links on a website? Which parts of our DNA correlate with a particular disease? LLMs like ChatGPT build on pattern recognition, but on an abstract level: they predict, based on the massive amount of text they have ingested, which words are most likely to appear together. ChatGPT's output is largely a probabilistic result of a gigantic computational effort. With reasoning models like OpenAI's o1 or DeepSeek's R1, LLMs have evolved beyond mere "stochastic parrots".[5] But statistical associations between words and large clusters of them remain their backbone.

When a system can identify patterns, such as how anatomical features like noses and eyes are arranged, it can also recognize them. It can categorize objects, matching individual people to a passport photo or spotting plants with early signs of disease, for example, but also how proteins fold, how global weather patterns evolve or how animals communicate. Pattern recognition can be used to predict things. Given its wear, is a truck tyre likely to burst soon? These predictions, if reasonably accurate, enable us to target resources better, so that we only use pesticide on patches of crops at risk of insect infestation, for example.

Once algorithms try to predict human behaviour, however, things get murky. Biases of all sorts enter the equation, as do threats of manipulation, surveillance and oppression. Algorithms pick up nefarious patterns of human behaviour just as much as those of which we are proud. Such issues might seem disconnected from our political economy focus. We disagree. Predicting human behaviour is a potential goldmine, and current AI developers are driven by profits. It may seem like an innocent technological advance when Amazon uses machine learning to forecast demand for "millions of products globally in seconds" (according to the self-indulgent portrayal by Amazon Web Services in a 2021 Forbes newsletter). But it might replace whole squadrons of data engineers who previously forecast demand, pile more pressure on warehouse workers to realize the quick delivery turnarounds machine learning promises, and tempt Amazon to record customer behaviour even more comprehensively and intrusively than before. Behaviour prediction and profit maximization make for an unsavoury mix. How AI becomes part of our lives is deeply inter-twined with the incentives its developers face.

As a form of applied data science, AI systems can also dynamically optimize processes. Here, the dynamic bit is new. Optimization itself – for example, finding the shortest route from Cologne to Amsterdam or Bucharest – existed before AI, as in car navigation systems. Those systems needed to be pre-programmed, however, and they used data from a virtual map. The AI ver-sion, in contrast, can learn from data it ingests along the way. Current road conditions suggest that we will run into a traffic jam in an hour? An AI helper reroutes us promptly.

The most prominent AI systems currently use neural networks. They have typically been trained on real-world data, such as text or images, but also uni-versity student CVs or weather observations.[6] The probabilistic equations in neural networks reflect the coincidence of things in the wild, for example in which contexts the word "orange" refers to the fruit or to a colour.

Reinforcement learning is different, not only in the underlying tech, but also in its data needs. Imagine you want to teach a computer a simple game, like Tetris. Our game-playing AI can "see" the blocks piling up on the screen, and it can push the game's left, right, and rotate buttons. Crucially, it can also see its own score, which goes up when a line of blocks is full and cleared. Now the AI is tasked to maximize its score, with no further instructions. We encourage it to try the buttons and figure out "what works". The first few dozen Tetris rounds are predictable disasters. But as by accident, our game-playing AI does something that increases its score and keeps the game going, it figures out when to push which buttons for success. That, then, is reinforcement: a system programmed to maximize a certain reward and but otherwise left to its own devices to figure matters out. When by happenchance things go well, the AI will do more of what it just did and, over time, it learns its tricks.

Used a lot in robotics, reinforcement learning features a key difference compared to the neural networks powering LLMs: the training data is generated as the system itself is developed. The AI needs no records of past Tetris games – forget about the huge data troves we commonly associate with training AI systems. This difference has important political economy implications. LLM developers have often bypassed ethical and legal boundaries to obtain data, frequently against the wishes of data creators. More recently, companies like OpenAI have cut expensive deals with high-quality content providers such as the *Wall Street Journal*, creating a competitive disadvantage for smaller model builders and reinforcing entry barriers in the LLM market. At the same time, such arrangements generate new revenue for companies outside the AI core, such as news organizations. In contrast, AITs with more modest data appetites (like the Tetris example) exhibit lower potential for market monopolization.

To make this discussion more systematic, consider some things that companies and people do with AITs. Our overview is by no means exhaustive, but it gives a sense of the most important kinds of AI. Generative AI has certainly attracted most news coverage.[7] But its quick diffusion and show-stopping capabilities have overshadowed other AI applications in public debate and imagination, obscuring the real economic impact less flashy forms of AI can have. Consider some examples.

Companies develop AI systems for business process optimization, many pre-dating the birth of generative AI (although they may now integrate the newer technology). The South African firm DataProphet, for example, built PRESCRIBE, a system to optimize manufacturing processes and to cut operational costs. The software sifts through production data, flags inefficiencies and suggests how to avoid production defects, energy waste or downtime. With only 43 employees and a single-digit million-dollar revenue figure in 2022, the company bets on further automation in manufacturing. As spending on AI in manufacturing "is anticipated to reach USD 16.3 billion by 2027" (a sevenfold increase in five years), CEO Frans Cronje dreams of making DataProphet "the leading provider of impactful AI for the machines that make the world".[8] Both the business model and the overconfidence are indicative of dynamics in this sector.

Other companies use AI not just to augment business processes but to replace them altogether. US-based Lemonade wants to overhaul the insurance market by automating customer interactions from contract signing to claim management. Kasisto, also from the US, lets AI handle customer conversations in banking. ServiceNow promises platform solutions to optimize workflows for everything from human resources management, customer services, information technology (IT) operations and service management, to supply chain management, cyber security and risk management, and in-house app development. This range of applications makes it difficult to speak of a specific ServiceNow AI product and its economic effect in the singular. Annual company revenues grew by almost a quarter in 2023 ($9.4 billion in April 2023) and it listed more than 22,000 employees in April 2024, quite something for a services firm hardly anyone outside the management world has heard of.

Consumer-facing apps, too, increasingly incorporate AI. Recommender systems built into apps like Yelp, Spotify, Tripadvisor or Bumble learn from user behaviour or feedback. Compared to generative AI, the actual tech behind the algorithms is relatively simple, and it does not require the quantity of resources necessary for something like ChatGPT. At the same time, scalability is high, and network effects loom large, not least because user data is proprietary. So whereas AI is central to how these companies recommend things and run their businesses, the basic market dynamics differ little from similar companies before AI proper made its entrance: think of concentration dynamics in pre-AI social media platforms. When we tease apart these dynamics in Chapter 3, we find entry barriers across many AI market segments, but the barriers themselves can vary substantially.

Fusing AI and robotics is a completely different offshoot of the AIT cluster. Manufacturing plants have used robots for decades. AI adds adaptability. Conventional robots, whether those on a car production line or those lounging around hotel lobbies as gadgets, are pre-programmed. AI-augmented robots can explore and internalize the layout of spaces in which they have never operated. With reinforcement learning, humans can train them to perform fiddly tasks, for example plucking petals off a tulip or folding garments. Computer vision combined with an improved representation of three-dimensional space allows robots to move autonomously, like drones navigating independently in the air or under water. Speech recognition and human language comprehension allow people to interact with robots more naturally.

Robots integrate AI into hardware in contrast to an LLM, which users can access through a whole range of devices. That offers robotics companies or traditional hardware manufacturers without a history in computing a piece of the pie. The Swiss company ABB is strong in AI-powered robots. The Chinese XAG markets autonomous agriculture drones, reporting collaborations across 63 countries and regions in 2025. US farm equipment maker John Deere has also bet heavily on digital technology as it jockeys for a leading position in "precision agriculture", promising farming "personalized at the plant level", as the authors of a case study put it without any obvious irony.[9] At the same time, startups like the Chinese 3S are entering the field, in 3S's case using AI to automate welding of non-standard steel modules like bridge components or ship hulls. Big Tech has poured money into AI-powered robots, too. OpenAI set up a robotics research group in June 2024; earlier that year, many of the largest US tech firms took large stakes in Figure, a US robotics company. Quite different companies jockey for competitive advantage in this field.

Some of the most eye-catching AI applications so far come from traditional robotics firms. Boston Dynamics claims that its robot dog Spot can assist teams "from factory floors to construction sites to research labs and beyond". Equipped with extremities reminiscent of legs, it uses trial and error, typical of reinforcement learning, to climb over a pile of rubble. Spot boasts 360-degree vision, speech, facial and object recognition. The algorithm that animates Spot learns from sensorial inputs and big data to let Spot navigate different terrains. The robot can detect radiation, gas or vibrations; it can read temperatures and gauges, and identify anomalies from predefined standards. The Italian police force reportedly uses Spot to inspect grave-robber tunnels under the ruins of Pompeii; the Japanese Fukushima municipality deployed it to measure radiation after the 2011 nuclear accident. In principle, Spot owners can mount all sorts of additional equipment onto it, including weapons. Boston Dynamics adamantly denies that Spot is to be used in this way. Whether such corporate policies can withstand determined governments' co-optation of tech for military ends remains to be seen; we certainly are sceptical. But even without lethal firepower, the use of robot dogs in US border and law enforcement has been controversial already.[10]

A final example of AI-powered technologies other than LLMs worth considering is biometric identification, especially FRT. Iris and fingerprint scanners are also widespread, especially in border control, and criminology may soon integrate DNA sampling in identification. For now, FRTs remain the most widespread identification technology, using cameras and computer vision, which has vastly improved with deep learning. Remote biometric identification raises many thorny issues and became one of the most controversial issues as EU politicians negotiated the 2024 AI Act: they can be used for surveillance and oppression, notoriously in China but also elsewhere[11]; they suffer from racial and gender biases; they can still make consequential mistakes; and to build them, companies tend to use images in ways that violate people's privacy.[12]

The influential Gender Shades study from 2016 found, for example, that gender classification systems often used in FRTs misrecognize dark-skinned women in more than a third of all cases, a shocking combination of bias and low accuracy when considering the use of FRTs for discipline and control (in this case, firms such as IBM, Google, or Microsoft use the classification to target advertisements to the perceived gender, to verify identities, or to tag people on social media).[13] Cognisant of global power asymmetries, critics count FRTs "among the most problematic modes of extracting data from Southern populations due to its invasiveness, automated nature, deep-rooted racism, and many flaws that are technological as well as ethical and legal".[14] Chinese smartphone maker and African market leader Transsion, for example, uses its patented "beautifying dark skin" technology – nominally a tool to counter the racial biases of US-made FRTs – to extract millions of dark-skinned images for the largest global database of its kind.

What sets FRTs apart from other AITs is their relative maturity and widespread use. While less than perfect and morally questionable, they are widely applied and seen as functional by governments and private security companies alike. There are no obvious areas for further radical innovation. FRTs can be integrated with other technologies, for example smartphones and payment systems (Japanese company NEC offers face-based payments throughout the 2025 Expo in Osaka). Like optical character recognition, development in this area has somewhat run its course. Here is a form of AI that is neither show-stopping nor booming, but rather an off-the-shelf, everyday technology like many others. Its useability for crime prevention and detection, population control and the oppression of oppositional groups or protesters has created a large public procurement market. Market dynamics for FRTs, explored in more detail in Chapters 3 and 6, are thus bound to differ markedly from those for generative AI.

More examples like this will be discussed throughout this book. But it is worthwhile reiterating that the AI hype covers only part of the AIT spectrum. Too often disagreements about the essential characteristics of AI or its consequences are rooted in the different forms of AI we have at the back of our minds. Next time you read an op-ed about AI, notice how, even though the term is used at that level of generality, the author usually implies a very specific version of AI, and thus how the whole argument about AI and its transformative impact may fall apart if the example used is not an LLM but a smart refrigerator.

From thinking machines to Big AI

Most histories of AI trace the field back to the middle of the twentieth century. In 1950, the English mathematician Alan Turing published *Computing Machinery and Intelligence*, detailing an "imitation game" (later known as the Turing test) for determining whether a computer could pass for a human. Six years later, Stanford computer scientist John McCarthy organized a research workshop at Dartmouth College, New Hampshire, with the aim of forging a field of research to "[build] machines able to simulate human intelligence".[15] At the workshop, AI as a field was handed its official birth certificate.

Many such historical accounts are hagiographies of "AI and its Inventors", rather than attempts to understand how what we know today as AI emerged from a complex knot of lineages, contingencies and rationales.[16] What happened in the mid-1950s was not a fresh start, beginning from scratch. Instead, the leading contributors to early AI development, including Marvin Minsky, Frank Rosenblatt and Herbert Simon, carried with them ingrained conceptions from management and operations research, cybernetics and related fields.[17] With these traditions came the assumption that human intelligence could be seen as a complex of mathematical and logical operations: a highly rationalist and individualist take on human intelligence, showing little concern for social context, our mind's embeddedness in physical bodies, or our consciousness. The spirit in which AI research began was one that prioritized control, manageability and order, not just open-ended curiosity and speculation about the mind and our ability to reproduce it. From the very beginning, governments developed and used statistics and data science to control and steer societies. And the same is true for computers.[18]

People have long realized that technological innovation can have massive economic impacts, and "intelligent machines" have been no exception. John Maynard Keynes' visions of the *Economic Possibilities for Our Grandchildren*, largely freed from drudgery thanks to machine helpers, is one of the more famous examples. Nevertheless, without massive computing power available, early research was mostly theoretical, musing about whether thinking machines would even be possible, what they might be able to do, and what kind of architectures they would need.

Early inventors did not have CEOs breathing down their necks, eager to commercialize the AI they were hatching. That did not make AI research a free-floating creative endeavour, however. The US government heavily supported initial AI research, including with \$2.2 million at the Massachusetts Institute of Technology in the 1950s and 1960s. First concrete applications like Joseph Weizenbaum's chatbot ELIZA caught wide attention. At the same time, AI research failed to spawn marketable products. Allen Newell and Herbert Simon's research on a General Problem Solver – a problem reduction system to process highly predefined logical problems – spanned several decades without yielding practical applications. By the early 1990s, financing shrivelled, researchers increasingly shunned the term "AI" and continued their foundation work under headings such as cognitive or intelligent systems.

Or so stories about AI summers (progress) and winters (stagnation) would have it. If progress means machines getting closer to human-like intelligence, then indeed little happened for long periods. In the meantime, however, computing developed rapidly and thrived with inputs from academics, public authorities like the Defense Advanced Research Project Agency (DARPA), large companies such as IBM and later software companies like Oracle and Microsoft. Burgeoning databases – often filled through the surveillance-based business models of platforms like Facebook and Google – were to expand AI's capabilities down the line. If we regard AI not as some mythical quest for an artificial form of human intelligence but as a branch of computing building algorithms for pattern identification and prediction, its historical trajectory looks different. Increases in transistor density on microchips, for example, have progressed with considerable regularity for decades. As LLMs depend on massive computing power to work, each step towards better computer chips or central processing units (CPUs) has also been a step towards AI as we know it.

There are other continuities between the evolution of AI and the broader digital economy, for example in its hunger for data. As it became traded, exploited and frequently monetized – a new "fictitious commodity" in Polanyian terms – data gained prominence as capitalism's latest fetish.[19] Scholars likened it to a raw material (like oil extracted from fossil reservoirs) or something cultivated (like crops on a farm).[20] Yet others portrayed data as analogous to land: a territory to be explored, mapped and enclosed like private property to generate rents.[21] Irrespective of which metaphor fits best, they jointly highlight how data access has been crucial for AI's technical and economic breakthrough.

Some types of data had monetary value and legal ownership long before the digital age. (Potentially tradable) patents granted exclusive rights to monetize inventions; copyright did the same for other creative works, such as books. Much casual creative output, such as recipes or photos shared on Facebook, fell under no solid copyright regime, however. Ownership and monetization of data, like other resources, depend on formal and informal legal structures.[22] Still, data has some quirky properties. Unlike consumables – an apple can be eaten only once – data can be reused indefinitely to train AI models. That raises the stakes for securing ownership over data, which requires significant legal barriers or what Kean Birch calls "data enclaves".[23] If data is a key AI ingredient and its use and ownership hang on legal regimes, training algorithms inevitably becomes a legal and political issue: under what conditions can companies access and utilize the necessary data? And what economic benefits, if any, flow back to its original creators?

Platform companies are great data hoarders, incessantly monitoring their users, shaping online experiences through personalized feeds and refining services based on patterns they have identified.[24] That said, we should not conflate the business models of platform companies and those building AITs. As we pointed out previously, forms of AI vary enormously, and only a subset of companies leverage user data as platform companies do. Not all AI producers can embrace extractivist and monopoly-seeking strategies.

The current discourse that "AI is new and revolutionary", therefore, overlooks how many continuities there are in and with AI and how it has grown out of deeply entrenched social, economic and political conditions, which allow some players to profit from publicly shared data. The field and its priorities are white and male-dominated, mirroring traditional racial and gendered hierarchies while hiding the groundbreaking intellectual work by female and Afro-American coders.[25] And like today, geopolitical considerations – the hope of using AI for military purposes, especially during the Cold War – have always lurked in the background. At different junctures during the second half of the twentieth century, the RAND Corporation became intensely involved in AI research; today, firms like Palantir, Helsing and Anduril provide AI-driven intelligence analysis tools, autonomous surveillance and defence systems to armies around the world.

Many enabling conditions were thus in place when AI regained prominence around 2010. Feeding on vast databases and hardware, neural networks trounced older systems at pattern recognition, computer vision and language processing. Large-scale commercial applications suddenly seemed realistic and funding for AI shifted: where previously universities and government agencies had been heavily involved, companies started pouring money into AI, turning the field into the Big Tech-dominated affair we know today.[26] Given the speed of events, it is easy to forget how, just a few years ago, in 2019, Facebook rechristened itself as Meta, convinced that the Metaverse (virtual reality) would be the next big thing. Only in early 2023 did Mark Zuckerberg announce that the company would shift its attention to AI after all.

It remains to be seen just how transformative AITs will be: we expound our more nuanced view in the chapters to come. In public debate, however, the hype has clearly prevailed. In 2023, the WEF suggested that three quarters of companies were prepared to adopt AITs by 2027, based on a survey with 800 business leaders across the globe.[27] McKinsey's 2024 "State of AI" report highlighted that almost three quarters of all surveyed companies were already using AI in 2024, up from 20 per cent seven years earlier, with over a third investing at least 5 per cent of their digital budgets in AI tech.[28]

Such claims should be filed under "sensationalism" and symbolic adoption practices. They suggest a shift in business practices that belies how shallow most adoption is. "Using AI" ranges from completely overhauling production and logistics to employees using Google's AI-powered search when they look something up – something that is hard to avoid by now. When the WEF surveys corporate leaders, which ones will seriously deny that AI may be of interest to their company? And can the sample of companies McKinsey queried be considered representative of both large and small businesses worldwide?

Other surveys, both academic and industry-based, indicate significantly lower AI adoption rates.[29]

That said, irrespective of whether the AI *transformation* will be as momentous as such reports claim, the current AI *boom* is real enough, fuelled by sky-high expectations and the funding that follows in their wake. As we show in Chapter 3, the computer science breakthroughs of the past two decades have been met with ballooning venture investment and, to a lesser degree, government funding. OpenAI alone raised $11 billion in venture capital in just five deals since its foundation, only slightly less than the EU startup scene in its entirety in 2021 ($13 billion) and certainly dwarfing historical investments in AI. In 2023, AI startups together raised more than $27 billion.[30] The AI-driven capital expenditures of four of the largest US tech companies (Alphabet, Amazon, Meta and Microsoft) more than doubled between 2023 and 2025 to reach over $300 billion.[31]

Much investment is speculative: a gamble on as-yet-unrealized (and often unspecified) future revenues. Nvidia's skyrocketing market capitalization has been exemplary, built mostly on expected sales of AI microprocessors. If those are bought by companies building AI capacity, then the implied revenues of AI companies, to justify all their projected capital expenditures, would need to hit $600 billion.[32] Considering that the revenue of the leading AI firm (OpenAI) is in the low single-digit billions, that revenue expectation is wildly optimistic, to say the least. Other companies in the field also reached unlikely market valuations seemingly out of nowhere. For example, OpenAI's implied market value surged to $176 billion in early 2025, up from $27 billion in 2023. In most other sectors, it simply would not be possible to build a company valued at more than a billion dollars from scratch in less than a year. It took Fei-Fei Li, an established figure in Silicon Valley, only four months to do so.[33]

The AI boom's speculative character bolsters the US and China as its epicentres. The American startup scene allows entrepreneurs with promising ideas and the right connections simply to try things out.[34] The venture capitalists funding such enterprises do not expect success every time. It suffices if every now and then one startup strikes commercial gold. There is much more "risk capital" available in the US than elsewhere, certainly compared to, say, continental Europe. The American political economy favours what Peter Hall and David Soskice called "radical innovation" over the "incremental innovation" which has traditionally thrived in countries like Germany.[35] Indeed, a consensus has emerged in Brussels that it is not a lack of good ideas that has hampered European innovators but the lack of opportunities to "scale up". Considering this funding angle, it is hardly surprising that "Big AI" has flourished especially in the US and also in China with its tradition of heavy government support for fledging sectors and national champions.[36]

With the need to scale, Big Tech companies enter the picture. They have both deep pockets and other digital offerings that complement AITs. They also control distribution channels – app stores, operating systems, cloud services, and so on – to bring AI to businesses and consumers en masse quickly. Many tech giants benefit from rather autocratic corporate governance structures: founders often are dominant shareholders, giving CEOs leeway to embark on risky executive decisions and costly U-turns.[37] When competition among AI companies is high, the ability to occupy and possibly corner markets is essential. It leaves little room for slower competitors, including those with more transparent governance. And it tempts companies to rush half-baked products out of the lab. Meta did so with Galactica, a scientific-article generative AI that excelled at fabricating nonsense; Microsoft had the racist Tay chatbot; Alphabet the Bard LLM, which was notorious for its misfires.

Fixed costs for generative AI are high, and marginal costs are low. Building an LLM for only one client is not significantly cheaper than one servicing a thousand. What is different, however, is the amount of hardware needed to build a cutting-edge model. At least until the Chinese DeepSeek stunned the tech world in early 2025 – claiming that it had beaten OpenAI's top model with a build of its own that had cost only a few million dollars to train – the industry consensus was that training a competitive model was prohibitively expensive, and that costs would only increase.[38]

Either way, compared to model building, inference (generating content from the finished model) uses fewer resources: namely, the hardware on which the AI runs, plus the energy costs to power it, including cooling ever more and ever larger data centres. In contrast to much other software, however, LLMs typically run "in the cloud", not on a user's device. The cost of inference is borne in the first instance by the model provider, so by a company like Alphabet. The environmental impact of model inference quickly outweighs that of model training when the number of queries run into millions every day.[39] With energy use not only a pollution source but also a corporate expense, inference certainly is not costless.

High upfront costs, easy scalability and potential scarcity of key inputs like the computing hardware create strong oligopolistic tendencies in the LLM market. First movers can secure substantial power. But how significant ingredients are to different AITs varies widely. Training Spot the robot dog does not need the football field-sized data centres that a foundation model requires. Systems that learn relatively slowly, as new data comes in, can take things one step at a time. A potential scarcity of top-shelf computer chips is not a major problem for them.

The same is true for using the model once it has been trained. Spot the robo-dog or 3S's AI-powered welding robot does its job just fine using its inbuilt or local computer, in stark contrast to the data centres into which ChatGPT queries are currently wired. The more hardware an AI application requires – robots are good examples, as are high-definition cameras for FRTs – the less extreme the asymmetry of high development costs and low marginal costs becomes. Even once Boston Dynamics knew how to build Spot, it still costs thousands of dollars to build another one. With a reported sales price starting at $74,500 in 2020, manufacturing costs are likely to be in the same ballpark.

The economic dynamics of the LLM market have been crucial in shaping the trajectory of a model-builder like OpenAI. The company found itself at a crossroads as the costs of training larger models, retaining skilled staff and paying remote workers for data labelling soared. In response, OpenAI shifted from a non-profit to a "capped-profit" model in 2019, limiting investor returns to 100 times their funding, a cap so high that the lab's costs are nearly identical to traditional for-profits. According to the lab, this move was key to securing the cash needed for computational resources and to attract top researchers in its quest to lead on creating safe and widely useful AI. However, venture capital investments often come with strings attached, such as pressure to deliver short-term returns which sideline more open-ended initiatives. OpenAI's business model shift paved the way for its pivotal partnership with Microsoft, which invested one billion dollars as the first step in a lasting collaboration. OpenAI gained access to immense computing power through Microsoft Azure but granted the tech giant preferential access to cutting-edge AI research in return, bolstering Microsoft's edge in the broader tech landscape. The marriage of AI and Big Tech as we know it today had been consummated.

The difficulty of political oversight

AITs and the companies developing them have become powerful. From a democratic perspective, that raises the question whether and how AI development can be subordinated to political guidance or control. As we show throughout this book, governments often have incentives to promote AITs: they promise gains in cost-efficiency in the public sector (illusory or not), have military uses and seem to offer productivity increases that might raise living standards and thereby please voters. AITs also hold many risks, creating a need for AI governance. Algorithms can reach enormous complexity, which render them inherently obscure and difficult to monitor. We cannot look under the hood of an AI model to find out why one loan application was rejected and another accepted and whether a decision was discriminatory. Was it the zip code? The sector of current employment? The high school attended by the applicant? Somebody's ethnic background or gender? All these factors combined? As things stand, we have no clearcut way of determining the relative weight of any input factors.

The complexity that makes political oversight necessary also renders it difficult. If the whizzkids building the algorithms do not fully understand what is going on within them, how can policymakers do so? Such informational disadvantage is a serious political problem: the politicians tasked with steering AI policy inevitably struggle to gauge both the potential and the risks of systems. Information asymmetries between industry experts and legislators (such as the risks related to tobacco or pesticides) have troubled other regulatory domains, too. But the challenge goes beyond simply understanding how an AI model functions. It is also about mapping the vested interests embedded in them, as well as the inequalities their deployment may generate, which often go unnoticed but can shape outcomes in ways that disadvantage certain socio-economic groups. These hidden dynamics complicate crafting effective and fair regulations.

In consequence, policymakers are vulnerable to manipulation from those who presumably know best: the companies developing the algorithms in the first place. The danger of regulatory capture looms large, particularly when the underlying models perpetuate or exacerbate existing inequalities. Because policymakers cannot survey what these systems can and will do, how much there is to win and lose and for whom exactly, the optimistic but self-interested arguments of AI developers have a high chance of carrying the day. That in turn pushes commercial impulses to the fore, whether of the anti-regulatory or protectionist kind. There are currently few economic sectors in which as-of-yet unproven narratives about our prosperous future feature so prominently.

Also in that respect, AITs vary widely. Compare impenetrable generative AI algorithms to remote biometric identification, like FRTs used in a central city square or at an airport. Few people understand exactly how these algorithms tell us apart even from close lookalikes. But what can be done with these systems and where potential problems lie is relatively easy to understand, not least because the tech has matured and its operational purpose is clear: visually identifying a person. This relatively easy-to-understand character of FRTs finds policymakers much less vulnerable to corporate lobbying, leaving relatively less room for commercial considerations to overrule the societal ones. For example, regulators in Brussels seem to have understood the risks of real-time mass surveillance through FRTs for democratic societies and therefore agreed to ban some of its uses, but they struggled to pin down what risks might come with the largest general-purpose models.

These knowledge dynamics are closely related to a second important feature: AITs have evolved quickly and many continue to do so. Even though the intellectual foundations of neural networks date back to the 1980s, the development of deep neural networks in combination with escalating computing power and data let the technology take off only in the 2010s.[40] Once its potential had been demonstrated, companies built ever larger training datasets, for example by scraping enormous amounts of images or text from the internet. In consequence, generative AI systems especially have vastly improved within just a few years. ChatGPT can easily be customized to avoid regurgitating stilted prose, writing in anybody's personal style instead. Where system capability is only a question of scaling (throwing more data or computational power at the problem), its evolution may still be relatively easy to anticipate. Other aspects of system performance are harder to predict.

The uncertainty surrounding the limits of AI's capabilities complicates matters further: if there are inherent limits, where do they lie? When algorithms learn from human-generated data about human skills, we should not be surprised to find that once competence matching ours is reached, progress levels off. How much better and quicker than a human can you get at telling apart cats and dogs? Maybe big strides towards vastly superhuman capabilities are nothing more than a naïve and unwarranted extrapolation of past performance increases? Similar worries about undue optimism surface with respect to learning from ever more data. The amount of digital content keeps growing quickly, and an increasing chunk is itself generated by AI. Will ballooning low-quality content degrade future LLMs, potentially to the point of collapse? Or can that problem be circumvented through careful data curation, for example by only using vetted, high-quality content?

AI developers have long harvested web data, routinely ignoring copyright concerns. This echoes long-standing practices in the technology sector like Google's book-scanning project, which drew lawsuits over intellectual property violation from authors and publishers alike. Access to first-rate data (pay-walled news, peer-reviewed papers) is limited and growing far more slowly than demand.[41] As a result, developers increasingly turn to data from lower-quality sources like social media, leading to biased or absurd outputs, like Google's AI Overview suggesting glue as a pizza ingredient. Many content providers from news organizations to platforms like Craigslist and Reddit restrict access to data scrapers. Lawsuits over intellectual property, like the *New York Times'* 2023 case against OpenAI and Microsoft for unpermitted use of its articles, signal an even broader pushback. In response, AI firms cut deals for data access, as OpenAI did with *Time*, *Le Monde* and Axel Springer SE, whereas others resort to scraping YouTube videos or social media posts, continuing to violate data protection laws such as the EU's.[42]

Even if tech development were to stall – by reaching the physical limits of computer chips, for example – the AI-powered transformation of economy and society would not stop, and the need for public scrutiny would not disappear.

There is a time lag between the invention of new technologies and their broad diffusion, let alone the moment all potential applications have been exhausted. Jack Clark has called this lag the "capability overhang" as a shorthand for any technology's unrealized potential.[43] This notion is important. Even if AI capabilities were to plateau, socio-economic transformations would be far from over and regulators would still need to monitor their undesired effects. This is less a question of what AI experts at OpenAI or DeepSeek can do, and more of innovators discovering progressively more uses for a mature technology. Kai-Fu Lee, the former head of Google China, has argued that AI diffusion is drastically different from its radical innovation phase, and whereas US companies excelled at the latter, it will be Chinese companies that create the seemingly more mundane but ultimately more transformative and lucrative real-world applications.[44] More recently, Jeffrey Ding has seen that diffusion advantage with the US, not China.[45] But both Lee and Ding agree that diffusing AITs through society and economy is the key to benefitting from them in the long run, rather than having had the original idea or invention. A political economy of AI must therefore go beyond the major players driving AI innovation and consider how these technologies spread, reshaping production, distributional dynamics and everyday life. We do so in Chapter 4.

All these debates illustrate how people disagree about the speed of AI development. Whoever is right, two observations stand out: the first is that there *is* genuine disagreement, even among people developing AITs or working with them daily. The simple truth is that we do not know where things will stand one or two decades from now. Second, just how much these dynamics matter varies enormously across different types of AITs. The hard-to-predict AI evolution makes anticipating the future impact of AITs inherently difficult, whether for citizens, businesses, governments, or for us as authors.

Where the speed of AI innovation is high, however, two additional dynamics kick in. First, people who are affected negatively (say, workers whose livelihoods evaporate) will struggle to anticipate changes and mobilize before it is too late. By the time specific consequences become manifest, it may be too late to address them through pre-emptive interventions. And second, opportunities for regulatory arbitrage generated by rapid innovation give tech developers a permanent route to circumvent regulation, even once public authorities have decided to regulate a specific application or use case. AITs constitute a particularly defiant target for regulatory interventions, tilting the balance of power away from public authorities.

One example of the problems posed by rapid and unbridled AI innovation is the critical yet often overlooked environmental impact of resource-intensive AITs. This starts with producing the necessary hardware, hinging on mining rare-earth minerals (often in China or parts of the Global South), which fuels exploitative and unsafe working practices and severe ecological damage like soil erosion and water contamination.[46] The environmental toll goes beyond metal extraction, however. AI data centres consume copious amounts of electricity and water. Cooling systems strain local water supplies; soaring energy demands overload ageing power grids, driving up carbon emissions and undermining broader climate goals. In 2024, Big Tech firms have reported emissions spikes exceeding 30 per cent, primarily driven by AI data centre expansion.[47] In response to rising demand, Microsoft plans to reopen the Three Mile Island nuclear plant – the scene of a major reactor meltdown in 1979 – whereas Alphabet is backing small nuclear reactors to power its AI businesses.

The scale of AI-related resource consumption can be staggering. Training OpenAI's GPT-3 alone generated over 500 tons of carbon dioxide. It is not just training a model that consumes resources: generating a single 100-word email with GPT-4 uses about half a litre of water.[48] Such models' resource intensity has alarmed activists and researchers, who have long warned about unsustainable patterns in AI development.[49] Yet again, AITs vary in their resource demands: an FRT, for example, is far less energy-intensive than Alphabet's latest LLM, if that comparison even makes sense.

Over time, advances in hardware production, algorithm design and data centre management could curb AI-related emissions. Some AITs help cutting waste and off-time in manufacturing and logistics, and they can make fossil energy extraction more cost-effective. Given such ambiguities, AI's environmental impact seems as little technologically determined as its economic impact. Throughout its history, the impact of AI has been a political issue, shaped by decisions on whether and which AI systems should receive funding, be adopted in public settings, be regulated more or less tightly, or be required to offset their environmental footprint rather than externalizing it to us all.

3

American AI and the Chinese challenge

AI is a moving target, and dominant narratives about its direction keep shifting. One day, massive data centres are the only way forward; shortly after, DeepSeek and edge computing seem to signal openings for smaller players. That AI would have a broad impact was already clear in the 2010s, as tech ecosystems in the US and China matured. But few political economists anticipated the speed with which AITs developed, especially generative AI.

Launched in November 2022, ChatGPT became the fastest-growing consumer application in internet history, reaching around 100 million users in only two months. Just like the Soviet satellite Sputnik in 1957, the chatbot fired the imagination of both the public and policymakers, showcasing to a wide audience just how capable AI had become. From writing Shakespearean sonnets on climate change to debugging Python code, ChatGPT's versatility triggered a surge in interest and investment in generative AI. This excitement, amplified by business and tech media and AI firms' self-promotion, quickly overshadowed other AITs. Established giants like Alibaba, Alphabet, Baidu and Meta soon competed not only with each other but also with new players such as Anthropic, Baichuan, Moonshot AI, xAI and DeepSeek in the rapid global expansion of generative AI. In the ensuing boom, the biggest winners have not necessarily been these new companies, but the "AI enablers" who control the resources that make AI possible.[1] These include US cloud hyperscalers, chip designers and manufacturers from Nvidia to TSMC, but also firms providing sensors or server hardware.

The global AI sector is heavily concentrated in the US, home to many companies across the AI stack from chip design to downstream applications. China has emerged as the main competitor in AI development, ranking second in terms of companies, investment, and highly skilled staff. With its gigantic domestic market, state-driven funding and top-down coordination of innovation initiatives China has become a formidable tech power. The US has tried to slow China's rise through export restrictions and limits on knowledge transfers. But ultimately, that has only encouraged Beijing to foster homegrown alternatives, and with success.

In this chapter, we concentrate on "AI-first" firms, meaning companies that sell AITs or access to them, or that are contributing to the production of AITs as a central component of their business strategies. These firms form the core of a rapidly expanding AI-intensive corner of the global economy, one shaped not just by market forces but also by state policies, geopolitical rivalry and techno-optimist narratives. Understanding how this core ticks and what drives or limits its actions is important for evaluating AI's wider ripple effects. We explore how the launch of ChatGPT shifted the global AI ecosystem, leading to a prioritization of resource-intensive generative AI and sparking increased competition among both Big Tech and startups worldwide. Broadening our scope to examine the US-dominated global AI stack, we can see how state-industry ties and patterns of market consolidation create distinct types of winners and losers, in turn enabling tech giants to tighten their grip on the digital economy. Shifting to China, we explore how state backing and strategic investments drive AI-first firms globally, with implications not just for Sino-American AI competition but also for countries in the Global South.

ChatGPT's Sputnik moment

Having partnered with Microsoft, OpenAI found itself standing on the shoulders of a tech giant. The AI lab had hit significant milestones in the years prior to launching ChatGPT in late 2022. Back in 2020, it introduced GPT-3, the biggest LLM ever built at the time. It was trained on a sweep of internet data, including both copyrighted and freely available material, and reportedly cost over $4 million to train – a modest amount by today's standards but staggering at the time.[2] Due to its scale and expense, GPT-3 became OpenAI's first closed-source model, with Microsoft securing exclusive access in return for providing investment and cloud infrastructure. Everyone else could only reach it through a commercial application processing interface. This helped OpenAI collect valuable usage data and generate revenues to offset its research and development costs. Early adopters like Reddit and learning platform Quizlet illustrated GPT-3's versatility, even as the model drew criticism for "hallucinations" (generating plausible-sounding but misleading or false results), issues that would resurface with ChatGPT.

OpenAI next expanded its GPT architecture into new domains with new kinds of training data. One notable result was Codex (the model behind GitHub Copilot), which generates code in response to prompts using knowledge pillaged from tens of millions of GitHub repositories. The lab also ventured into image generation, first with Image GPT and later with DALL-E, which created plausible if frequently surreal visuals. Launched in 2022, DALL-E 2 quickly became an internet hit, reaching a million users in just three months. Its sharper image quality sparked both viral memes and a wave of anxiety, with artists raising red flags about their work being scraped without credit or pay. Some celebrate DALL-E for democratizing content creation, but fears of labour devaluation and AI-driven job loss complicate this narrative. The same is true for code-writing AI: tools like GitHub Copilot might help some junior workers transition into more advanced software development.[3] But such progress is built on large-scale pilfering of human-written code, and it can degrade developer jobs over time. Commercially driven firms, which control the development and use of AITs, ultimately shape how AI is implemented, often in ways that may limit its positive social impact.

Then came ChatGPT. Built on OpenAI's foundation models and Microsoft's cloud muscle, the chatbot was celebrated by media outlets as a catalyst for AI-driven transformations across industries and professions. Although early critics flagged issues like bias and misinformation, the launch marked a turning point. No other product before had propelled AI into mainstream consciousness so fast or forced Big Tech to scramble so hard to catch up. In response, Alphabet released its chatbot Bard (later rebranded as Gemini); Meta prioritized AI development over its ill-fated Metaverse, doubling down on open source models; and Amazon secured partnerships with AI labs while expanding its in-house toolkit. The frenzy around resource-intensive generative AI overshadowed both other kinds of AITs and smaller generative models designed for more specific purposes.

As users flocked to ChatGPT, investment followed. OpenAI, still earning little revenue, abruptly became one of the most valuable US startups. By January 2023, its valuation soared to $29 billion, more than double its worth just two years earlier. That same month, Microsoft cemented its partnership with OpenAI through a $10 billion investment allowing the tech giant to integrate OpenAI's models into products such as its Bing search engine and Office applications like Outlook and Word. Fearing mounting pressure on its core search business, Alphabet rushed out Bard in February 2023 to a botched launch that wiped $100 billion off the firm's market value, about 9 per cent of Alphabet's market capitalization at the time. Such stock price rollercoasters became common in the post-ChatGPT boom, feeding on mood swings in market sentiment. They only abated somewhat when other developments, like hostilities in the Middle East and Trump's announcement of enormous tariffs, started to dominate economic news cycles and alternative future scenarios.

The 2023 launches of OpenAI's GPT-4 and Alphabet's PaLM models marked the emergence of a new market; foundation models, which are giant LLMs capable of handling a wide range of tasks. OpenAI's and Alphabet's foundation models have been trained with immense datasets, computing power and financial investment. Research institute Epoch AI estimates that the costs of training foundation models have more than doubled annually since 2016, driven by increasing expenditures on advanced AI chips, skilled staff and energy consumption.[4]

Extrapolating such trends, training a single cutting-edge all-purpose model could well have exceeded $1 billion by the end of the 2020s.[5] As it turned out, however, LLM development does not follow a straight line: in early 2025 Chinese DeepSeek shook markets with its R1 model that matched OpenAI's leading systems in performance despite being open source and reportedly developed at a fraction of the cost. Simultaneously, several initiatives succeeded in training capable models using computing capacity distributed over several clusters, opening the way for decentralized LLM development. For now, however, any focus on building resource-intensive LLMs reinforces the dominance of tech giants that control the requisite cloud infrastructures, whereas the real diffusion of generative AI in practical business applications could well rely on smaller, more resource-efficient models.

Foundation models share important economic characteristics with platform businesses like Facebook and Google, for whom scale, continuous data accumulation and network effects drive growth and market power.[6] But there are also important differences. Platforms often engage in data capture, achieved by maximizing user engagement, cross-subsidizing non-profitable but data-rich business segments, or acquiring competitors to expand market share.[7] With large AI models, computing is more critical for a competitive advantage than data alone. Training data is easier to access than ever before, whether through web scraping, proprietary business data, paid access to curated content, open source repositories or synthetic data.[8] On top of that, Big Tech has deep pockets, expert staff and massive cloud infrastructure, creating the right conditions for the creation of Big AI. Data matters, but it certainly is not the only critical resource.

AI's growing ties to big business were on full display in Sam Altman's firing and reinstatement as the CEO of OpenAI in late 2023. The company had started out as a not-for-profit committed to developing AI for the betterment of humanity. The board ousted Altman, concerned about a lack of transparency and an increasing hunt for profits. His dismissal sparked an internal outcry, however, with over two-thirds of the lab's loyal staff threatening to resign while Microsoft offered to hire Altman and any disgruntled employees. Under mounting pressure, OpenAI's board had little choice but to reinstate Altman lest most of its employees leave. With that move, the company had solidly settled on a commercial course.

This episode reveals the tension between profit-driven innovation and safety precautions, particularly when major investments are at stake and unbridled AI development is framed as central for competitiveness. The board's decision to bring Altman back exposed deep flaws in OpenAI's governance, which ultimately crumbled under the weight of economic interests. OpenAI's new board, instated after the failed Altman ouster, featured financial capitalists, tech moguls, ex-military figures and corporate philanthropists. It too showed the deepening entanglement of established market forces with tech development within the leading AI firms.

More generally, the Faustian bargain between AI labs and Big Tech – where the former trade control over their innovation pathways and product commercialization for access to financial and computational resources – has followed three main routes: corporate acquisitions, financial investments, and strategic partnerships.[9] Especially in the US, Big Tech has long used mergers and acquisitions (M&As) to strengthen business lines or enter new markets, consolidating resources like property, staff and physical assets.[10] In contrast, financial investments and partnerships allow firms to access growth opportunities, diversify risks and earn extra revenue without the regulatory and organizational intricacies traditional M&As entail.

By 2024, tech giants like Microsoft, Alphabet, and Amazon had collectively spent over a quarter trillion dollars on M&As and investments, roughly the cost of NASA's entire Apollo programme when adjusted for inflation.[11] Notable AI-related M&As include Microsoft's $19.7 billion purchase of speech recognition firm Nuance Communications in 2022 and Amazon's $1.2 billion acquisition of autonomous vehicle maker Zoox in 2020. During the early 2020s, increasing regulatory scrutiny and a more robust antitrust policy suppressed Big Tech M&As as companies faced tougher approval processes and legal challenges from institutions like the US FTC, the European Commission, or the British Competition and Markets Authority. In response, Big Tech employed new strategies to consolidate AI dominance while sidestepping regulatory scrutiny.

One favourite has been the "acqui-hire": snapping up startups primarily for their human capital. In practice, that means buying small firms not for their products or customers, but simply to hire their teams. For example, in 2023 Microsoft absorbed AI assistant maker Inflection; Amazon brought in AI agent developer Adept; and Alphabet took over chatbot creator Character.ai. These deals attracted scrutiny from American and European trustbusters alike, yet antitrust investigations were ultimately dropped, particularly after more assertive regulators like Lina Khan and Margrethe Vestager left office. Big Tech walked away largely unscathed, and in March 2025, Alphabet even closed its largest-ever acquisition, buying cybersecurity company Wiz. It was a clear sign that the appetite for tough antitrust policy had waned under Trump's second administration.

Strategic partnerships with AI labs have only cemented Big Tech's dominance. Microsoft's mentioned alliance with OpenAI grabbed headlines, but even its smaller €15 million investment in French startup Mistral, touted as Europe's answer to Silicon Valley AI, sparked sovereignty fears in France.[12] Alphabet and Amazon funnelled $6 billion into OpenAI rival Anthropic, securing early access to its LLMs. Apple, a relative latecomer to the AI game, struck a different kind of deal: it integrated ChatGPT's capabilities into its proprietary AI system dubbed "Apple Intelligence". Instead of a financial investment, it offered OpenAI exposure to customer data through hundreds of millions of Apple devices. Amba Kak and colleagues rightly concluded that Big AI is effectively "owned by Big Tech".[13] The technologies may be new, but the companies that dominate them have ruled in the digital space for decades already.

Concerns from regulators and policymakers over market concentration have promoted open source AI, hailed by some as a way to democratize access and drive innovation. The share of open source AI models has grown over time, with around a third of newly released foundation models in 2023 being open source, including DeepSeek's headline-grabbing releases.[14] By letting independent developers, researchers and businesses build on existing frameworks, such tools lower entry barriers and accelerate AIT diffusion. And it is not just about LLMs: open source AI is also gaining momentum in areas like computer vision and robotics. For example, the Gazebo robotics simulator enables users to model and test robot populations in intricate environments, much like a videogame engine.

Unsurprisingly, leading firms like OpenAI and Google AI tend to keep their best LLMs closed, citing risks like disinformation, cyberattacks and deepfakes. Even so, open source AI is thriving. Platforms like Hugging Face and Alphabet-owned TensorFlow have become notable hubs, whereas open-access LLMs from Mistral and Meta are gaining traction. Meta's Llama models, built to run on many different hardware and cloud systems, boost accessibility and flexibility. Llama 3 (released in April 2024) reportedly rivalled top-tier proprietary models from OpenAI and Alphabet, as did DeepSeek's V3 and R1 models on their release. In such cases, open models take direct aim at the closed counterparts of market leaders to chip away at their dominance. Still, what counts as "open" varies: some firms release model weights, keeping training data under wraps. While a step towards greater openness, this still falls short of real transparency. And behind the open source branding, tech giants like Meta and Alphabet extract value from unpaid volunteer labour while reinforcing their dominance by setting the very standards the rest of the open ecosystem must follow.[15] We return to the promises and perils of open source AI in Chapter 7.

The launch of ChatGPT in late 2022 intensified global AI competition. In China, major actors like Baidu, Alibaba and Tencent ramped up LLM development. This required balancing heavy investment and domestic regulations aimed at curbing political dissent, as well as mounting geopolitical pressure from US export controls.[16] Initially introduced during the first Trump presidency, these restrictions gained bipartisan momentum, with both the Biden and the second Trump administration broadening limits on exports of advanced chips like Nvidia's A100 or H100 graphics processing units, as well as chipmaking tools from firms like the Dutch ASML.

Baidu's Ernie chatbot – launched in March 2023 after four years of development – kicked off a "war of a hundred models" in the words of a senior Tencent executive.[17] Rivals like ByteDance and Moonshot jumped in, competing through both rapid innovation and aggressive pricing. But China's AI ambitions stretch far beyond chatbots. Baidu's Apollo project advances autonomous driving; iFlytek and Transsion lead in voice and facial recognition. Companies like Baichuan and Borns Robotics move into AI-driven healthcare; robotics firms such as Siasun, 3S and Unitree Robotics are scaling rapidly by tapping into China's status as the world's largest market for robotics.[18] This surge in Chinese activity has for now turned AI development into a two-horse race for global AI leadership.

This bipolar AI landscape is complicated by development of AITs elsewhere. Across Europe, Asia and the Middle East, states and businesses invest in AI research and development. European startups like Mistral, Aleph Alpha and Stability produce LLMs and image generators; a company like DeepL refines neural network-based translation tools. In India, firms such as Glance build personalized shopping feeds, whereas South Korea's Trillion Labs focuses on Korean-language LLMs. Meanwhile, Gulf States like Saudi Arabia and the UAE are betting big on AI to diversify their economies for a post-oil age, with the Emirati model-builder G42 forging ties with Microsoft.

This global momentum reflects a push for tech influence beyond the usual superpowers. How successful that will be remains an open question as business models and customer demands evolve: will there be a dedicated market for "homegrown AI" in countries outside the US and China, possibly pushed by protectionist governments? To what degree will customers want or need access to top-tier AI, giving leading firms a lasting advantage, or be content with "just good enough" products? And how much can current AI leaders lock customers into their products, for example by leveraging proprietary distribution channels (operating systems, cloud infrastructure and so on)? We will return to these questions throughout the book.

Unpacking the US-dominated AI stack

Seeing how the launch of ChatGPT has reshaped priorities in AI development, it is helpful to take a step back and dissect the broader funding mechanisms and tech stack underpinning the AI ecosystem. This connects to our earlier argument: AI does not just reside in virtual models; it is financed and built across a wider digital industry. Dominant digital companies not only have enormous financial resources but also control key infrastructures and expand vertically into AI applications across industries.

Over the past decade, corporate investment in AI has risen steeply, turning AI from a niche research area into an envisaged driver of innovation and growth. Initially concentrated in the information and communications technology (ICT) sector, AI investment has expanded across other industries like finance and retail.[19] Finance going to non-publicly traded firms – AI labs like OpenAI and Anthropic, as well as numerous startups – made up over half of global corporate AI funding in 2024.[20] The US has attracted the lion's share of such private investment, at more than 70 per cent. The post-ChatGPT hype around generative AI is also evident: about a quarter of private investment in 2024 ($33.9 billion) went into this kind of AIT. Adding to the spending spree, Big Tech firms poured over $150 billion into AI-related data centres, chips and servers between mid-2023 and mid-2024. Their preponderance in AI funding and infrastructure shows a growing power concentration, giving a few major players huge influence over the direction of AI innovation. In the meantime, the question whether these investments will really pay off continues to lurk uncomfortably in the background.

When it comes to which kinds of AITs get financed, data from the Organisation for Economic Co-operation and Development (OECD) shows that, as of 2025, the top three AI-related startups worldwide by funding are mobility and autonomous vehicle firms – China's Didi Chuxing ($28.5 billion raised), Uber and Cruise – rather than companies focused on generative AI.[21] In Germany, Aleph Alpha trails behind Celonis, an AI-driven data processing platform used by firms like Bosch, Citibank and John Deere that has raised $2.4 billion across six deals compared to Aleph Alpha's $638 million. This pattern holds in many places around the world. In Indonesia, France and Nigeria, top AI firms specializing in finance and insurance, logistics and retail, or business processes have attracted more investment than well-known LLM developers. Although ChatGPT's Sputnik moment shifted investment priorities, the broader AI ecosystem remains much more diverse. The Celonises of the world matter: if AI applications like insurance platforms or surgical robots turn out to operate in markets driven less by speculation and more by tangible returns on investment, their economic impact may be considerably underestimated at present.

State funding and procurement also play an important role in shaping AI development, even more so where market incentives fall short. While corporate investment in AI vastly exceeds public funding, it follows presumed opportunities to turn a profit, often neglecting the needs of marginalized communities. This is where public authorities can step in, not only by commissioning specific products, but also by funding basic research to increase AI systems' reliability, safety and fairness. Public investment can therefore steer AI towards delivering social good.

Tracking public AI spending is notoriously difficult, but several metrics offer insight. US public AI research and development funding has risen steadily since 2018, reaching $1.8 billion in 2023, with significant allocations to agencies such as DARPA, the National Science Foundation and the National Institutes of Health.[22] Since 2022, US federal AI contract spending has surged, focusing heavily on defence and security applications.[23] Similarly, China directs public AI investment through its New Generation AI Development Plan. In contrast, the EU's funding for AI development, mainly through initiatives like Digital Europe and Horizon Europe, has been relatively limited, which is an important factor in understanding Europe's current standing in the global AI landscape. Other nations, including India, Japan and South Korea, have bolstered their AI infrastructures through similar strategies, even if they remain clearly inferior and subordinate to those in the US or China.

Government funding has supported US firms' global dominance. Washington's National AI Research Resource launched a two-year pilot in 2024, aiming to provide researchers across the US with access to computational resources, data and AI models. The final report proposed a $2.6 billion budget for the first six years, with most allocated to funding "advanced computing resources as well as data, training, and software resources".[24] In practice, and betraying the Valley's widespread libertarian attack on public interventions, considerable US taxpayer money flows to a handful of already powerful Silicon Valley companies in exchange for access to their near-monopolistic data infrastructures, computational resources, clouds and software. These kinds of tit-for-tat deals have only intensified since Donald Trump reassumed the US presidency. Big Tech firms also sponsor research centres, chairs and graduate programmes at universities or hire professors under dual affiliations. Altruistic as this might look, such sponsorships risk co-opting independent AI researchers into corporate agendas and undermining their autonomy.

Big Tech has also built a large lobbying machine to bend regulation and policymaking in its interest. In addition to protecting self-regulation in the initial phases of the recent AI summer,[25] firms have successfully watered down several regulatory projects. Tech companies' sway over national policy waxed further in Trump's second term. In the initial days of his mandate, the president signalled a shift towards unbridled AI development with minimal regulatory oversight (prominently with the Stargate Project to boost US AI infrastructure or his repeal of AI safety rules established during the Biden era); in return, he has demanded (and has so far received) Big Tech fealty to his "Make America Great Again" agenda.

The Corporate Europe Observatory has evidenced how US Big Tech influence reaches across the Atlantic: Meta, Google, Apple and Microsoft were among the top lobbying spenders in Brussels in 2023 according to the EU Transparency Register (along with Bayer and Shell), jointly spending €25.5 million (the whole tech sector's EU lobbying cost reached €113 million in 2023).[26] And this lobbying translated into access: in 2023, 86 per cent of the meetings high-level officials of the European Commission held on AI matters were with industry, with Google representatives meeting "three commissioners in just one day".[27] In addition, the recruitment of Commission officials into Big Tech firms, or the law firms advising them, has become a widespread strategy for bolstering privileged positions. In one striking example, "the former antitrust official Nicholas Banasevic joined Microsoft to lead its competition and regulation team" in 2024 after having "led the Commission's attempt to crack down on Big Tech's abuse of its monopoly power".[28]

The AI stories tech companies tell have shaped both policy debates and investment decisions. The performative nature of these future-oriented narratives can be most clearly seen in post-ChatGPT financing and research priorities, with investors frequently backing AI firms based on anticipated market power rather than actual returns. This speculative dynamic has hurt stock prices of companies seen as lagging in AI (such as Apple or Intel). It also triggered major stock volatility following disappointing events, including Nvidia's 2024 second quarter financial results, which, despite strong growth, failed to meet investors' sky-high expectations. In January 2025, DeepSeek's R1 model once more exposed the fragility of speculative investment narratives, challenging the prevailing consensus that LLMs' performance hangs on massive infrastructure spending. US tech stocks collectively shed $1 trillion in market capitalization in response.

Among the so-called "Magnificent 7" tech stocks (Alphabet, Amazon, Apple, Meta, Microsoft, Nvidia and Tesla) those that had positioned themselves as "AI-first" have seen their market capitalization grow most between 2020 and 2024, specifically Alphabet, Meta and Microsoft. Nvidia, however, stands apart: its valuation has soared more than tenfold during this period, making it one of the most valuable corporations in the world in mid-2025. Meanwhile, private AI labs like Anthropic and OpenAI have also reached staggering valuations. OpenAI saw its market value jump from $29 billion at the beginning of 2023 to $300 billion by April 2025 – more than 23 times its estimated annual revenue.[29]

No surprise, then, that pundits have warned of a speculative AI bubble, which raises concerns among economists and investors should the hype not translate into real growth.[30] Between October 2023 and June 2024, over half of the S&P 500's market capitalization gains were driven by Big Tech and chip companies like Broadcom, Qualcomm and Nvidia.[31] Nvidia alone accounted for nearly a fifth of these gains, lifting not just the tech sector but the entire US market.[32] Between March and June 2024, virtually all S&P gains were tied to "companies touched by AI".[33] The AI hype sustained market momentum even amid a broader economic downturn. At times, concerns over returns on AI investments trigger swift reactions in stock markets, with investors dumping large volumes of tech shares virtually overnight in a bid to pre-empt losses from their high-risk bets. Is the post-ChatGPT AI hype a financial bubble, and if so, when will it burst, and what will its impact be on the global economy? At stake here are not just stock market portfolios, but a whole economic model and hierarchy that has AI companies and innovation perched at the very top.

To better understand how this economic model works, we need to unpack the AI stack – not to predict if or when a bubble might burst, but to grasp market dynamics unfolding across the different layers of the AI economy. At the very surface we have the companies developing AITs, such as LLMs, AI-powered robots and FRTs. They rely on AI enablers – firms involved in areas like resource extraction, chip design and manufacturing, submarine cables and data centre infrastructure. Then, there are the companies that adopt AITs, integrating them into their operations or using them to create new products. In practice, these categories frequently overlap. For example, management consultancy firms replace some of their staff with AI and simultaneously sell AI adoption advice to other companies. When pursuing vertical integration strategies, AI enablers use their market power to expand across different parts of the AI stack. Alphabet is designing its own Tensor processing units to compete with Nvidia in AI chip development, and major cloud providers offer specialized AI services to third parties, from text-to-speech conversion (Amazon Polly) to image processing (Azure AI Vision). So far, most stock gains have gone to AI enablers and providers, suggesting that AITs have yet to see widespread adoption across the economy.

Focusing on the financial bottom line, there is an enormous gap between the revenue growth generated by selling AITs and the anticipated returns from AI infrastructure investments. Even if AI startups, along with US and Chinese tech giants, rake in billions from provisioning their AI systems, there would still be a shortfall of up to half a trillion dollars.[34] OpenAI, for example, doubled its monthly revenue between late 2023 and mid-2024 (reaching around $280 million) while Anthropic projected an annual revenue of $850 million for 2024.[35] These figures do not indicate profitability. Exact numbers are often confidential, but many AI firms, particularly LLM developers, probably still operate at a loss. Anthropic was reportedly burning through $2 billion annually by April 2024; Stability AI, known for its Stable Diffusion image generator, was expected to end 2024 with a $36 million loss.[36] Big AI is, above all, a big gamble on the future.

That said, not all AIT providers lose money. Outside the hyper-visible LLM domain, companies in other applications are turning a profit. Defence-focused AI firm Anduril reportedly retains over a third of its revenues after covering labour and computing costs, benefitting from contracts with institutions like the US Department of Defense.[37] Similarly, Chinese voice recognition firm iFlytek and British AI cybersecurity company Darktrace generate net incomes. Financial data for many developers remains scarce owing to their private ownership, but available information suggests that profitability may be more sustainable for firms specializing in targeted AI applications. Some AI domains suffer from worrisome hype, others much less so. Nuance matters.

Neither is AI provision the exclusive domain of startups. Established firms, both in the US and beyond – Alibaba, Spotify or Indian conglomerate Reliance Industries – also offer proprietary AI services to businesses and consumers. Since the launch of ChatGPT, these companies have enjoyed substantial revenue growth, even if it remains impossible to pinpoint how much of this growth is directly linked to AI provisioning, as these figures are often kept private or lumped together with broader cloud revenue numbers. For Alphabet, Amazon, and Microsoft cloud computing has been one of their fastest-growing revenue streams, even if profitability differs. In their 2024 quarterly earnings, American tech giants hailed AI as a major growth driver, signalling to investors that investments in AI infrastructure were starting to yield tangible returns.

The surge in cloud revenues among US hyperscalers shows the growing demand for digital infrastructure, but not everyone is convinced that this growth is entirely organic. Investors and financial journalists have raised concerns that part of the boost may come from "round-tripping", when Big Tech firms fund AI labs only to see that money return as payments for cloud services.[38] Regardless of how real the demand spike is, Big Tech's push into both powering and providing AITs reflects a deliberate strategy to tighten their grip on the digital economy. The cloud sector itself is an oligopoly, with just three US companies controlling over two-thirds of global supply.[39] Competitors like Alibaba, IBM, Oracle, Salesforce and Tencent remain on the fringes, although domestic providers dominate in markets like China. The capital-intensive nature of cloud computing locks in Big Tech's dominance and makes it exceptionally hard for new entrants to break into either AI infrastructure or cloud provisioning. Even if it is no iron law, the tendency is clear: market dominance is self-reinforcing unless someone throws a spanner in the works.

AI enablement goes beyond cloud. It encompasses hardware, from silicon chips and data storage to servers and data-collecting sensors. Here, the biggest beneficiaries are companies whose products are essential for LLM training, especially high-performance chip designer Nvidia and leading chip producer TSMC. Designing and manufacturing these chips requires enormous capital investment, access to cutting-edge photolithography machinery and highly specific human expertise – scarce resources that restrict competition and enable a handful of firms to dominate. Efforts to expand production, such as President Biden's CHIPS (Creating Helpful Incentives to Produce Semiconductors) and Science Act, take not just billions of dollars but extensive lead times, as semiconductor factories take years to build and reach full capacity. Geopolitical restrictions reinforce market concentration, with governments actively intervening in the race for scarce AI hardware. Under US pressure, the Dutch government barred ASML from exporting its most advanced chipmaking tools to China, tightening Washington's grip on the sector and pushing Chinese semiconductor firms to seek workarounds and accelerate domestic alternatives. In China, AI developers turned to less powerful chips, black-market Nvidia tech, code optimization, or homegrown hardware – Huawei, for example, has claimed that nearly half of all Chinese LLMs were trained using its Ascend chips as of mid-2024.[40]

Nvidia lies at the centre of the AI hardware ecosystem not just as a chip-maker but as the force behind the CUDA (Compute Unified Device Architecture) software, a proprietary platform that enables developers to write code so that applications run more efficiently on the company's chips. This also makes it costly and technically unwieldy to switch to other hardware, turning Nvidia into a chokepoint in building AITs and attracting antitrust scrutiny worldwide. Despite growing interest in technical alternatives – such as Alphabet and Amazon's custom chips and the increasingly powerful hardware made by Chinese Huawei – Nvidia's lead remains difficult to dislodge. Compounding this bottleneck is the AI industry's reliance on TSMC for fabricating advanced chips. With the bulk of the company's operations based in Taiwan, that company has become a geopolitical powder keg: any disruption would send shockwaves through global tech supply chains, hitting not only Nvidia but everyone involved in building electronics.

The Chinese contender

Contesting US dominance, China has spent the past decade nurturing a domestic market for tech innovations. But its trajectory as a major AI power has been far from uniform. Business–state relations under China's unique socio-economic system are complex, and AI-first firms differ in how they balance catering to the government's demand for certain technologies (such as FRTs) with developing commercially viable products for a large consumer base both at home and abroad. As we discuss further in Chapter 6, the entanglement of economic interests with geopolitical ambitions (often framed in decolonial language about strengthening technological autonomy in the Global South) further complicate this picture.

Nevertheless, initially cautious but increasingly assertive, Chinese state leaders have implemented economic governance strategies that, combined with somewhere between 700 million and 1 billion digital consumers, prepared the ground for tech startups to become globally competitive.[41] AI development has been a natural extension of this strategy. The Chinese government's thirteenth five-year plan (2016–20) promised "breakthroughs in artificial intelligence" such as the 2017 launch of a deep learning lab, led by Baidu, as part of a broader push to solidify China's AI position.

Bold state-backed investments in the sector have paid off. Between 2014 and 2017, China's IT industry produced 34 "unicorns", private companies worth more than $1 billion.[42] In the decade leading up to 2024, China ranked second only to the US in the number of newly funded AI firms, with 1,605 compared to the US's 6,956.[43] The two countries also dominate AI investment flows. According to OECD data, venture capital funding in AI remains overwhelmingly concentrated in the US (peaking at $114 billion in 2021), but China follows with a still remarkable $52 billion in the same year.[44] AI venture capital investment from 2013 to 2024 shows distinct funding priorities across China, the EU and the US.[45] China's investments are heavily concentrated in autonomous vehicles, robotics, sensors and IT hardware, AITs closely tied to industrial and mobility innovation. This focus has only marginally changed post-ChatGPT, with growing investments in IT infrastructure, alongside continued interest in social media and healthcare applications. Notably, investment in consumer-facing products only gained significant traction in 2024 despite having been marginal for years. In contrast, the EU displays a more service-oriented profile, with rather modest investment in robotics and mobility. Most EU funding flows into business processes, finance, and insurance, with IT infrastructure gaining prominence since 2022. The US shares China's emphasis on infrastructure and mobility, but it seriously lags in robotics. American investment is more evenly spread, with notable activity in healthcare, social media and the financial sector. Overall, these patterns suggest a strategic divergence: China prioritizes industrial and mobility-related AITs, the EU leans towards services and finance, whereas the US blends infrastructure and application-driven investment across high-value domains.

China's AI strategy goes beyond AI-first companies, aiming for a self-sufficient "red stack" spanning the whole digital ecosystem[46] – an effort accelerated by Biden's and Trump's export restrictions on advanced technology. Before these bans, semiconductors were China's top import, with $350 billion spent in 2020 alone. Firms like Huawei and SMIC depended on American and European suppliers not only for finished chips but also for critical manufacturing equipment such as ASML's photolithography machines. Faced with an increasingly strict US trade policy, China has poured trillions of yuan into domestic chip production. The unexpected success of China-based SMIC in producing 7 nanometre chips in 2025 signalled progress despite the sanctions. Companies like Alibaba and Baidu develop their own AI chips to reduce reliance on foreign tech, and Huawei by now offers chip clusters to train AI models that, it claims, match Nvidia's in performance.[47]

Restrictive US policy had limited foreign tech companies' access to Chinese markets, which benefitted local contenders. The catch-up development model of the "Great Firewall" has combined protectionist strategies and the scale of China's domestic market to create a predominantly inward-oriented digital economy.[48] Early movers in AI development also benefitted from aligning with the government's surveillance focus. For instance, Hikvision's FRTs have been used in discriminatory policing, with applications specifically designed to identify Uighurs.[49] YITU's Dragonfly Eye had been celebrated already in 2018 as the world's largest image database, containing 1.8 billion photographs, winning tech awards in the US, and enabling world-leading FRT development including for the purposes of repression.[50]

That said, the common assumption that China represents a purely state-capitalist, authoritarian model of AI innovation is too simplistic. Transnational capital flows and private investors have long played an important role in the emerging state-directed tech economy, well before China's government formalized the Digital Silk Road under its Belt and Road Initiative. Attracted by the large Chinese market, foreign investors have spent billions on AI development since the mid-2010s. China surpassed the US in AI venture capital funding for the first time in 2016, attracting $22 billion compared to the US's $17 billion.[51] By 2018, both countries were nearly equal at $33 billion before the US overtook China again, fuelled by the emerging boom in generative AI. This surge in Chinese AI investment led consultancies like PwC to encourage global investors to turn their attention (and cash) towards the "silicon dragon".[52]

A dynamic startup scene developed in China, with many entrepreneurs having studied abroad, particularly in the US. Their global networks, top-notch scientific training and familiarity with both Silicon Valley and local markets have given China's tech hubs a competitive edge. Some of China's most influential firms, such as Meituan, Baidu or the FRT giant YITU, were founded by entrepreneurs educated abroad, and a quarter of all Asian startups led by US-educated founders were based in China as of 2017.[53] In the early stages of China's ICT boom, private firms and local authorities alike were less focused on the government's push for "indigenous innovation", adopting and adapting foreign technologies and business models instead.[54] Only as these firms matured did they move from copycat strategies to developing their own innovations, especially in e-commerce, digital payments, FRT and more recently generative AI. US restrictions on Chinese students and workers only accelerated this shift. By 2020, China surpassed all other countries in AI-related research output and patent filings.[55]

The Chinese tech sector mirrors the US in its market concentration, with e-commerce giants like Alibaba and Pinduoduo, social media and gaming powerhouse Tencent and search engine Baidu dominating their respective niches. These companies aggressively pursue corporate funding and M&A strategies to entrench their market power and shape China's startup scene, not unlike Alphabet or Meta. In contrast to American Big Tech, the Chinese variant also reflects the country's unique political and legal context to produce distinct modes of scaling, which often involve intricate funding relationships between firms and strategic restructuring practices.[56] Leveraging such scaling efforts, players like Huawei and Xiaomi have come to dominate the domestic smartphone market and innovate in AI-driven biometric applications. However, Chinese Big Tech remains much smaller than its US counterpart. In early 2025, Tencent, the largest Chinese tech firm, had a market capitalization of around $600 billion – less than 6 per cent of Apple's, the world's most valuable company at that time. Despite domestic dominance, many Chinese tech giants struggle to expand globally (especially without proper government support), often due to regulatory pressures, international competition or reliance on local markets, all compounded by geopolitical tensions.

In the early phase of China's tech development, unparalleled access to data paired with the largest consumer base on the planet provided firms with a formidable edge. Boasting "1 billion internet users with a penetration rate of 71.6 percent" in 2021, China's digital ecosystem became a goldmine for collecting data and training algorithms.[57] Nevertheless, growing concerns over privacy and data security, especially after high-profile scandals and breaches, have pushed China to tighten regulations. Rules like the Data Security Law and the Personal Information Protection Law now restrict how firms collect, store and use personal data. These primarily target the private sector (especially foreign companies because of data localization requirements) whereas the state retains generous data access. Such asymmetric enforcement entrenches the government's role in AI development and expands its capacity for surveillance-driven governance, while still favouring domestic tech players.[58]

This initial concentration of market power in China's tech sector occurred not simply *because of* but in more complicated interactions *with* the country's state-directed model of economic governance. It was only in 2016 that the State Council and the Communist Party's Central Committee took a more proactive role with an ambitious ten-year strategy pledging 2.5 per cent of GDP in public and private sector investments.[59] Such state support was tempered by a regulatory crackdown in the early 2020s, when Chinese authorities launched high-profile antitrust investigations and issued record fines against major domestic tech firms, seeking to curb their newfound powers and rein in disorderly market competition.[60]

The wish for government control and encouragement of private initiative have frequently pulled tech development in opposite directions. We should thus not conflate Chinese tech companies with the Chinese government. Like their Western counterparts, these tech giants and startups operate in the context of global capitalism, navigating struggles over intellectual property, patent wars and competitive pressures, not just against other Chinese firms, but also against foreign players like Alphabet or Samsung. For instance, Transsion "considers its FRT patents for darker skin tones as 'weapons of competition' in preparation for a future smartphone war in Africa", primarily against Huawei and other Chinese rivals.[61] This positioning mirrors broader data-extractive practices and aggressive intellectual property battles *within* digital capitalism rather than a distinctively Chinese version of Big Tech. And as one should expect, Chinese tech firms have entered the global lobbying arena, not least because US and EU officials remain wary of their entreaties.

And yet, Chinese international AI expansion is not merely a business strategy. It is deeply politically shaped. The Digital Silk Road finances digital infrastructure projects across Southeast Asia, Africa, Latin America and the Middle East with a dual goal of boosting market shares for Chinese firms and promoting Chinese tech standards through digital diplomacy. Such efforts have propelled Chinese firms to dominate global FRT exports. Brookings reports that 45 per cent of China's export deals for these technologies involve autocracies or weak democracies, with key importers including India, Singapore, the UAE and Indonesia.[62] Chinese providers like Huawei and CloudWalk already command much of the FRT market in Botswana, Egypt, Ghana, Kenya, Nigeria, South Africa, Uganda or Zambia.[63] Between 2009 and 2021, Chinese tech companies secured 144 contracts for "safe city" or "smart city" surveillance projects worldwide.[64] That said, whereas much public discourse frames Chinese tech as serving primarily authoritarian regimes, Chinese-made FRTs are also used in European countries and the US.

China has made significant progress in other AITs during the post-ChatGPT boom, as well. Tech giants like Alibaba and Baidu, along with smaller firms such as 01.AI, Baichuan and DeepSeek, have developed LLMs often comparable to US competitors' best models. Baidu's Ernie 4.0, for example, attracted over 200 million users as of April 2024.[65] In 2025, Chinese startup Butterfly Effect launched Manus, touted as the first general AI agent, drawing considerable attention for its performance and versatility. These advancements signal China's rising prominence as a global AI leader – a narrative often reinforced by innovation-focused accounts that frame AI development as a two-horse race between China and the US. But should we assume that these breakthroughs will automatically translate into sustained and widespread economic growth?

In his book *Technology and the Rise of Great Powers*, Jeffrey Ding argues that past tech revolutions did not benefit the nations that pioneered innovations most, but rather those that successfully scaled and integrated them across their economies.[66] From this perspective, despite its proven innovation capacity, China has struggled to broadly incorporate digital technologies throughout its economy – particularly in traditional sectors like mining, construction or agriculture – due to a notable diffusion deficit. This deficit is rooted in an insufficient skill infrastructure that could leverage such technologies effectively: insufficient human capital, weak institutions for facilitating tech transfers between scientific centres and business, and limited trade openness. While China's large public sector provides a strong market and financial backing for specific technologies like FRTs, this alone does not resolve the broader diffusion deficit.

As a result, despite making strides in adopting consumer-facing tech in areas like e-commerce, Chinese businesses trail "behind the U.S. in penetration rates of many digital technologies across industrial applications, including digital factories, industrial robots, smart sensors, key industrial software, and cloud computing".[67] Taking a longer perspective, other analysts are more sanguine. Entrepreneur Kai-Fu Lee, for example, argues that whereas the US holds a clear advantage in AI development, China will ultimately lead in applying such technologies to commercially successful products, citing the country's large data pool and rapidly growing computing infrastructure.[68] Recent research shows that while China continues to lag behind the US in tech diffusion, the gap is indeed closing quickly, driven by strong public sector demand, consumer applications and the manufacturing sector.[69]

These perspectives do not have to be mutually exclusive. What emerges is a more nuanced picture: China's innovation system has become highly effective at developing and commercializing certain technologies as well as scaling them within targeted areas, while continuing to face barriers in their economy-wide diffusion. Whether China can overcome these limitations – either through ongoing state support, business-led growth or a mixture of the two – will ultimately determine its ability to convert its position as a scientific power-house into sustained productivity gains and global technological influence. In this sense, the AI race is not simply about who gets to innovate first, but who can integrate best, a topic we explore further in the next chapter.

4

Uneven effects across and within sectors

As more and more businesses seek to integrate AITs into their operations, any discussion of the political economy of AI diffusion must start by asking: why are these technologies spreading in the first place? The answer is less obvious than it may seem. AI is often hailed as the next great technological revolution, following in the footsteps of the steam engine, electricity and the internet – each redefining how the world works, connects and produces. But as we will show, it may just as much be used to redistribute value that is produced elsewhere, leaving overall productivity levels largely untouched.

AITs offer cost savings and productivity gains wherever patterns can be analysed and predictions made. Such broad applicability makes it difficult to predict AI's impact across businesses, industries or regions. By the same token, estimating AI-driven gains in aggregate indicators like GDP remains a dubious enterprise. Still, the debate offers valuable insights. If AI's economic benefits accrue in knowledge-intensive sectors, gains will probably amass in countries in the Global North. Meanwhile, nations reliant on labour-intensive industries – like agriculture, mining and manufacturing, particularly in Africa, Asia and Latin America – and especially those with cheap labour are poised to see fewer advantages. Such uneven distribution extends beyond national economies. Much as digital platforms altered the geography of value creation and capture both locally and globally, the impact of AITs will vary across industries and regions.[1] AI diffusion deepens integration within the global political economy by linking diverse industries into a novel tech ecosystem. But it also creates new divides and reinforces existing ones. The gap widens between industries thriving on AI and those struggling to adapt, between firms with the requisite financial, technical and human resources and those without, and between business functions that undergo AI-driven restructuring and those left unchanged.

Differences in AI adoption and its benefits reflect each sector's sensitivity to such technologies. Some industries are more receptive because of their data-driven nature, existing tech infrastructure or accumulated expertise, whereas others face hurdles from tasks that are difficult to automate, often requiring tacit knowledge, human intuition or empathy. These disparities are not just about technical feasibility; they also reflect political choices (such as public investment priorities) and entrenched global economic hierarchies. Even within industries, AI adoption can change hierarchies between firms. Dominant corporations and agile startups alike can harness AI to consolidate or gain market power, securing first-mover advantages and benefits from cross-sector integration. The gap between AI leaders and laggards in turn shapes competition and the direction of innovation: which types of technology are prioritized, and which ones are being neglected? Who stands to benefit from such innovations, and who is excluded or rendered dependent on systems developed with entirely different contexts in mind?

This chapter explores how AI restructures industries, frequently reinforcing existing inequalities while generating new ones. We examine what drives AI adoption, critically look at expected returns on investment and analyse sectoral differences in AI uptake from finance and manufacturing to logistics and agriculture. And we zoom in on intra-sectoral dynamics, where firms with access to capital, data and skilled workers consolidate market power, capturing greater profits and rents at the expense of their competitors.

Who really gains from adopting AI?

The textbook answer as to why economic agents develop and implement new technologies (whether a plough or a microchip) is straightforward: technology increases productivity by enhancing output per worker. But there is another possibility. Technology may not boost output but redistribute value in favour of capital owners. Whether this refers to systems that check how many coffee breaks employees take, measure how long a worker takes to make a widget or monitor drivers' delivery times, these are not just productivity trackers, but tools used to penalize workers who do not meet output expectations. Here, tech is not about improving productivity in the way a tractor replaces a horse but about exerting greater control over production by tightening the screws on labour.

The redistributive dynamic is not limited to disciplining labour (a topic we return to in Chapter 5). Other systems increase competition between economic agents, allowing their owners to skim off more surplus value. Many digital business platforms work this way. Uber, for example, pits drivers against each other for rides, creating an environment in which the firm and customers (who pay less for each ride) benefit whereas drivers absorb most of the uncertainty and expense. Booking.com does the same for hotel owners. Conceptually, this distinction between productivity-enhancing and purely redistributive innovation is important. In the first case, tech advances create value: a bigger pie that, at least in theory, could be shared between employers and workers, making everyone better off. The second scenario is a zero-sum game where gains for one party come at the direct expense of another. The societal benefit of such innovation is questionable at best.

Even when innovation does increase productivity, it is still an open question who benefits. How are the spoils of innovation distributed? Public debate typically glosses over this question. Mainstream discourse presupposes that technological progress is inherently positive and deserves full support, so long as it does not blatantly violate fundamental rights. Hyperbolic AI champions tag a similar line (just reread the first epigraph to this book by Marc Andreessen). The 2024 Draghi Report calls for Europe to boost its competitiveness, uncritically celebrating innovation as if its society-wide benefits are a given. That it might only benefit the few and even tighten their economic grip on the many remains outside its purview.

The techno-optimist obsession with productivity also remains agnostic about what we want to produce more of. Does churning out cheaper throwaway toys or accelerating fast fashion count as progress? Given the planet's dire ecological state, such indifference to the moral value of production is hard to defend. Even as AI can optimize natural resource use, its environmental net effect can still be destructive when it enables the production of more in less time, drilling deeper or pushing mass consumption to new heights through ever more effective salesmanship.[2] People's ideas about where the line lies between valuable, pointless and harmful innovation will differ, but there can be no doubt that all three exist.

Substituting machines for humans also changes the character of what is being produced in creative fields. If we reduce these to mere content production, then generative tools like ChatGPT and DALL-E can certainly generate images, text or music. But art is more than just its final form; it is about human expression and meaningful communication with others. To our mind, these are activities that deserve protection, as they matter to human flourishing.[3] A perspective that values only the monetary worth of output misses that whole point. As AI spreads across the creative industries, it not only undermines artists' earning capacities but also devalues creative labour itself, eroding the case for investing in artistic education and narrowing the space for human creativity.

Pundits and governments uncritically embrace innovation and productivity gains, leading them to support innovation with unwarranted enthusiasm. This techno-optimist bent is especially evident in predictions about AI's economic impact which assume that new use cases will naturally emerge as the technology evolves. Analyses that draw on micro-level productivity data paint a more pessimistic picture. Acemoglu, for instance, estimates that AI will contribute only about a 1 per cent increase in global GDP over the 2020s.[4]

Such predictions do not just describe potential futures passively at a distance; they actively shape investment behaviour, potentially through self-fulfilling prophecies. If firms and governments buy into optimistic projections, they may double down on AI-related expenditure and reinforce the hype cycle. Pessimistic takes, like Acemoglu's, can have the opposite effect. In the summer of 2024, investor fears over AI's uncertain economic impact contributed to a major sell-off in tech stocks, showing just how fickle AI investment remains.[5] Speculative futures, rather than concrete economy-wide gains, continue to drive much of the AI economy.

AITs can uncover patterns in large datasets to create new products, improve processes and boost productivity. But they can also generate predictions about economic actors – such as their preferences, behaviours, or willingness to pay – that allow them to be exploited more effectively. Boosts in digital productivity may simply mask value extraction as efficiency gains. Instead, AI creates informational advantages for its owners, allowing them to squeeze workers or firms elsewhere in the supply chain and extract value they did not create – a dynamic that Birch calls "parasitic innovation".[6]

An indicator like GDP conflates these distinct functions into a single metric: as long as revenues or cost reductions can be traced back to AITs, they are counted as contributing to economic growth. This dynamic is eerily reminiscent of how megabanks were hailed as engines of economic dynamism in the run-up to the financial crisis, despite their reliance on speculation and rent extraction. With financial sector incomes uncritically counted as productive in GDP statistics, the parasitic nature of many financial innovations only became clear once the damage was done.[7] Similarly, AI-driven gains can inflate GDP figures while masking underlying market distortions and systemic risks.

In the long run, a binary distinction between AITs as either value-adding or value-extracting is unduly simplistic. AI is double-edged as its impact depends on how, where and by whom it is adopted. Amazon offers an illustration: AI optimizes its logistics, for example, by placing frequently ordered items closer in warehouses, which enhances operational efficiency. It can also refine pricing strategies to maximize profits, ensuring that prices are just low enough to drive purchases. This does not create additional value but shifts it from competitors and consumers to Amazon, which exploits its pricing power and squeezes rivals that lack AI-driven insights. Thus, when a business uses AITs to make money, where that money comes from deserves close attention: is it value creation or appropriation? From the outside, that distinction is not always obvious.

For that reason, we need to take a closer look at specific AI applications. Those that are obviously used for value appropriation deserve less political support than those that really benefit society or the economy at large. This distinction also opens the door for more targeted political interventions. Many current policies uncritically support AI firms, taking their revenues or investors' excitement as proof of their contribution to the economy. Instead, where AI is simply appropriating value authorities might countenance legal interventions, such as banning predatory pricing. Rather than treating AI as a universal driver of growth beneficial for all, we must examine how it is adopted in specific contexts and whether it lives up to the grand promises that surround it.

Differentiation and integration between sectors

According to McKinsey's 2024 "State of AI" report, 72 per cent of surveyed companies reported having implemented AI in at least one business function, up from 20 per cent seven years previously.[8] Within a year, the number of respondents that claimed to have integrated generative AI into their operations doubled. We are well-advised to take such figures with a grain of salt. It is tempting for business leaders to inflate their AI usage in order to appear innovative in the eyes of investors and corporate board members.

The path from superficial AI adoption to integrating it meaningfully into business processes is arduous and complex. As we pointed out previously, "AI usage" is itself a diffuse term, spanning everything from automating core processes to employees occasionally querying chatbots or filtering emails with Microsoft Copilot. Many studies, such as those from the BCG consultancy and academic researchers, find lower adoption rates than the McKinsey report suggests. Challenges to capitalizing on AI investments include incompatibility with existing processes, insufficient AI literacy and budget limitations.[9]

So why do firms across industries continue to invest heavily in AI, even if returns are uncertain? According to Stanford University's AI Index report global investment in AI totalled nearly $190 billion in 2023, equivalent to about half of South Africa's GDP in the same year.[10] Much of this funding is fuelled by speculative beliefs in AI's economic potential, often amplified by myths propagated by tech gurus and policy officials alike. In this sense, the post-ChatGPT AI boom has clearly been driven by hype – expectations spark investment, which in turn fuels excitement, further expectations and a fear of missing out. In the meantime, a major part of the economic returns flow to AI enablers such as Nvidia, Amazon or Alibaba.

We witness meaningful AI adoption across business functions like human resources, marketing and inventory management.[11] In human resources, half of the companies surveyed by McKinsey reported cost reductions from generative AI, with 15 per cent even seeing substantial decreases. On the revenue side, AI has driven growth in areas like supply chain management and IT. For instance, a company like Walmart can use generative AI to create dynamic inventory optimization scenarios, improving its demand forecasting and accelerating the restocking of shelves, driving revenue growth.

In contrast, McKinsey sees "analytical AI" (essentially all non-generative AITs including content recommendation systems, robotics or FRTs) used especially for revenue generation rather than cost reduction.[12] This suggests that analytical AI adoption is more focused on creating value than capturing it from elsewhere. Its cost efficiencies are found in functions such as customer care and software engineering, whereas its revenue benefits are most prominent in marketing and sales, where 71 per cent of respondents reported growth. Additionally, a BCG report reveals that the highest economic returns for so-called AI leaders come from integrating these technologies into core functions like operations, marketing and research and development, rather than focusing on automating support functions such as customer service, IT or procurement.[13] AI use then leads to sustained value creation through strategic integration into business functions lying at the heart of a firm, rather than peripheral or support activities.

This means that firms can realize tangible value from AI adoption beyond cost-cutting or isolated pilot projects. But doing so requires what we can call *deep adoption*: major overhauls of production processes, paired with investments in tech and workforce enablement. Deep adoption involves redesigning workflows, securing or outsourcing computing resources, integrating new software systems (from data processing platforms to business analytics dashboards) and hiring more (and different) staff. In contrast, *shallow adoption* – such as dabbling with pilots that do not scale up or automating narrow tasks – may yield temporary efficiency gains without significantly changing the underlying business model. Few companies have the means to pursue deep adoption, which is why less than 5 per cent of the firms in the BCG report quoted previously have scaled AI across functions to achieve substantial returns. In theory, AI adoption promises economic gains, but in practice, organizational constraints and industry dynamics create a gap between potential and reality. These uneven starting points can widen intra-sectoral disparities.

To gauge variable AI diffusion across industries, many economic studies assess AI's future impact by breaking jobs into discrete tasks and evaluating how easily the latter can be automated based on technical feasibility alone. While we return to the limitations of this task-based approach to assessing AI's effects on labour in Chapter 5, it remains a common starting point for estimating patterns of AI diffusion. For example, workers in logistics, office administration, manufacturing, legal services and finance have been identified as most at risk of automation in the US and Europe.[14] These sectors are thus "AI sensitive".

Beyond automation sensitivities, some industries (advertising, ICT or pharma) are better positioned to benefit from AI thanks to existing technical infrastructure, expert staff and extensive datasets. The fossil energy industry is a good example. Advanced AI tools help discover new offshore oil or gas reservoirs and optimize robotic systems to drill deeper, creating additional revenues.[15] On a smaller scale, we see similar dynamics in agriculture and related sectors, where AI-driven insights into weather patterns, crop health and animal behaviour can be exploited commercially. John Deere uses AI on large agricultural datasets to optimize pesticide use and boost crop yields, turning its data holdings into a hard-to-replicate competitive advantage.[16]

Here then is a first reason why theory-driven estimates of AI sensitivity do not fully align with real-world AI adoption. High upfront costs for large-scale AI systems or uncertain returns on investment deter firms from deep adoption, especially where labour is cheap. Strong labour unions can resist job automation and governments have the power to impose AI restrictions to mitigate societal disruption. Although such measures remain limited, we have seen concrete examples, such as Italy's temporary ban of ChatGPT in 2023 over privacy concerns. Such political and economic factors vary across industries and countries and complicate the direct translation of "AI sensitivity" into actual tech adoption.

The picture gets more complex once we consider the variety of AITs and their regulatory environments. A firm can integrate off-the-shelf technologies like voice or facial recognition software relatively easily, whereas a customized chatbot trained on vast amounts of internal data demands far more resources and expertise and cannot be easily scaled. Cultural and regulatory contexts also matter. Ethical and privacy worries have influenced the EU AI Act's tough stance on remote biometric identification. Safety concerns have slowed the rollout of so-called "level 4" autonomous vehicles (capable of operating without human intervention under certain conditions) outside the US and China, where cities like San Francisco and Wuhan have allowed limited trials. Meanwhile, China's AI regulations impose strict controls on LLM outputs about politically sensitive topics. The EU also has generative AI restrictions, although these typically target hate speech and disinformation. Both regions regulate AI outputs, but their focus reflects different political priorities.

Beyond regulation, governments influence (and typically promote) AI adoption through industrial policy tools like research and development funding. In January 2025, the US Department of Health and Human Services announced plans to establish itself as a leader in healthcare AI applications through infrastructure development, data sharing, standard setting and public-private partnerships.[17] The UAE's *National Strategy for AI 2031* prioritizes other sectors: natural resource extraction, logistics and tourism, doubling down on local competitive advantages.[18] France has invested around €600 million to accelerate "automated road mobility", with a 2022 action plan envisaging up to 500 automated passenger transport services by 2030.[19] These strategic pushes reflect the market segments in which countries lead, or aspire to do so, as well as the political clout specific sectors have in them. Depending on a sector's existing strength and how deeply states can invest in its promotion, we should expect global ripple effects, like China's role in the global security and surveillance sector, which rests on its mass production and export of FRTs.[20]

States also influence the uneven adoption of AITs across sectors when they act either as powerful purchasers or developers of AI systems. Over the past decade, governments have hailed AITs as radical public service enhancers, promising accuracy, speed and effectiveness. Applications include chatbots to manage large volumes of citizen interactions, automated casework for detecting social security or tax fraud, smart diagnostics in healthcare, predictive policing, risk assessments for child abuse, live traffic regulation, facial recognition and biometric identification at borders, dialect recognition in asylum claim processing, and also military applications.[21] With this range of applications, the European Commission early on singled out the public sector as a key market for homegrown technologies, even if so far it has shied away from a hard "buy European" policy.[22] Reports of ill-fated pilots, failed rollouts, discriminatory and simply illegal use cases suggest that states overstate the real impact of AI just as much as business leaders.[23]

Irrespective of the excessive optimism about AITs' impact on public services, governments vary enormously in their "AI readiness".[24] We again take such rankings with a modicum of scepticism, but they do show substantial differences between countries. For example, in an Oxford Insights index the US leads with over 87 out of 100 points followed by Singapore at more than 84 points, whereas EU country scores range from just under 80 (France) to just over 50 (Croatia). Brazil, Chile, Uruguay, India, Turkey and Uzbekistan all outperform most Eastern European nations. The gap widens even further for Sub-Saharan Africa, where all countries except Mauritius, South Africa and Rwanda score under 50, and many even below 30. Given the infrastructure and investment required, for many countries the question is not whether they want to digitalize and how, but whether they can.

Hidden beneath these scores lie marked geographical differences in states' ability to command (or at least navigate) an AI supplier market that effectively aligns with their goals. A 2024 UK report on AI procurement highlights a structural imbalance between local government and industry both in terms of tech-related knowledge (can an AI system do what the provider promises in line with national laws?), pricing power and possible vendor lock-ins.[25] Public policy priorities can easily lose out. If this is a worry in the UK with its relatively large domestic tech sector, what do public procurement teams in less tech-ready and less affluent countries have to contend with?

Variation in economic resources on hand, labour market structures and state-level capacities mean that AI adoption will pan out very differently. Data confirms such differences across industries within single countries, and they often defy economists' predictions based on sectoral AI sensitivities. Take truck-driving: once seen as one of the first jobs ripe for automation, truck drivers remain in high demand in many places due to technical, regulatory or infrastructural barriers.[26] A US Census Bureau study found the highest AI adoption rates in ICT, education, real estate and finance, whereas logistics, hospitality and mining lagged behind.[27] Manufacturing and trade, including wholesale and retail, fall somewhere in between. The EU and China show similar trends.[28] An OECD analysis also including countries like Israel, Japan and South Korea shows even greater variation in AI adoption across sectors, although ICT consistently leads.[29]

Extensive AI use in ICT and finance should come as no surprise. These sectors have long used data-driven decision-making. That can benefit greatly from AITs' predictive and generative capabilities and allow easy implementation. Google, for instance, uses algorithms like PageRank to sift through and rank billions of webpages, boosting those linked to by other popular or important sites. The ICT sector has been a natural leader in digital innovation, not least because this is where most AITs have originated.

In finance, leveraging firms' data on everything from daily customer expenses to minute stock market fluctuations, algorithms now drive trading decisions, manage investment portfolios, evaluate customer credit risk and search for fraud and money laundering in ways unimaginable decades ago. Many financial institutions let AI assistants handle the bulk of their customer interactions. AI can also link financial firms more closely: for example, banks and insurance companies can use their data-rich interactions to automate underwriting and claims processing and to customize risk management.

Both ICT and finance are foundational sectors in the global economy, providing the digital and financial plumbing across industries. Firms in these two sectors have accumulated enormous amounts of data, built extensive tech infrastructures, and employed a large share of the world's leading computer scientists – important bottlenecks in developing and adopting AITs. Their financial power, reflected in high profit levels and market capitalizations of giants like Broadcom and Bank of America, allows them to invest heavily in AI experiments, from developing in-house systems to buying off-the-shelf products.[30] When these experiments are successful, economic power cements economic advantage.

AI adoption in manufacturing commonly lags ICT and finance, as the sector is already permeated with robotic systems that handle repetitive tasks in areas like automotive and electronics production. In contrast to digital-only environments, implementing AI in manufacturing faces added challenges owing to task complexity and unpredictability. Algorithmic quality control systems can easily detect defects in standardized assembly lines but tasks such as handling irregularly shaped materials or adjusting to sudden equipment failures require greater adaptability from AI systems.

The drive to automate manufacturing began in postwar America, where General Motors introduced the first hydraulic welding robots. Since then, robotics has become a fixture in factories worldwide. Counterintuitively, such legacies can obstruct AI integration into production lines that are already heavily automated, as it would require replacing heterogeneous machines – many of which come with inconsistent data-capturing methods – and substantial staff retraining.[31] OECD data on venture AI investment by economic sector confirms this dynamic: it shows a highly varied picture rather than a neat correlation between pre-AI automation and investment now.[32] AI venture capital prioritizes speculative, high-potential applications over those with a history of automation. The prospect of radical disruption appears to beat that of gradual but unglamorous product improvement, although, in practice, much of AI's transformation of manufacturing may proliferate through incremental integration.

Contrast this with industries like agriculture, which face even greater barriers to implementing AITs. A key problem is the scarcity of high-quality, representative data, often due to inconsistent and fragmented data collection.[33] This hampers development of fully autonomous machines, where unforeseen situations can trigger life-threatening automated decisions. Resistance to change also matters, especially in sectors that rely on entrenched working methods or tacit knowledge. Although in agriculture, for example, farmers are generally open to smart technologies, many remain hesitant because of a lack of user-friendly designs and accessible training resources.[34]

Resistance to AI implementation is intensified by limited understanding and mistrust among both managers and workers, who may worry about job losses, budget cuts or losing control over operations.[35] Concerns about AI safety and reliability (especially in high-stakes areas like food production or global supply chains) only deepen these fears. While resistance is often fragmented and context-specific, it shows that AI diffusion is not a frictionless affair; implementation can be delayed, deflected and at times even blocked.

In human-facing sectors like education, healthcare and tourism, ethical concerns and regulatory hurdles can slow down AI adoption. In healthcare,

AITs have made strides in diagnostics, administrative tasks and personalized treatment. However, tight budgets and data privacy laws such as the US's Health Insurance Portability and Accountability Act impede their diffusion. IBM's Watson Health, a company designed to assist doctors with diagnoses and treatment suggestions, faced major setbacks due to trust and performance issues, before ultimately being sold off. In education, AI-powered learning platforms adaptive to individual students' needs face barriers including a lack of funding, data protection and fears of sidelining human teachers.

Such imbalances in AI adoption not only deepen technical and economic disparities between sectors but also encourage greater integration across industries wherever new synergies can be exploited by powerful companies. Industries that adopt AITs more swiftly, or those better positioned within the AI ecosystem (thanks to their capital, data and staff) may branch out into new business areas, in much the same way as platforms expand into different product markets to grow their data holdings.[36] Big Tech's recent moves into the energy sector are an extreme example. Tech giants like Microsoft and Alphabet use their experience to offer AI tools for energy grid monitoring and optimization to other businesses. For instance, SunPower, the US solar energy provider, has partnered with Google Project Sunroof which collects data on global solar panel adoption among private consumers to create software that helps homeowners and businesses design their own solar panel systems.[37] Expanding renewables make the electricity supply less predictable, and the nodes on the electricity grid that can function as both suppliers and users of energy proliferate (including households and electric vehicles). Smart grid management becomes increasingly important and both its operation and keeping track of flows for financial accounting are complicated and data-intensive exercises – just right for tech companies.[38]

Beyond Big Tech, creative sectors like publishing and film own valuable human-created content that they can license to AI developers to generate new revenue. Hospital patient data is attractive to health tech companies. Whether they are permitted to monetize that, and in which form, hangs on legal frameworks. Japan, where legal frameworks are lax (particularly around copyrighted material), has attracted AI firms eager to scrape digital data for model training – much to the dismay of local creatives.[39] Consultancies like McKinsey or Deloitte also capitalize on the AI hype with strategic guidance, implementation support, and customized AITs for businesses lacking in-house expertise. BCG reported that AI-related consultancy work accounted for a fifth of its revenue in 2024.[40]

The cross-sector integrative effect of AI adoption is likely to be stronger with larger, more generalist AITs, such as LLMs which typically require large and diverse datasets for training. Just as many companies opt for cloud computing instead of proprietary hardware, they may hesitate to buy specialized AI models if a tech company like Baidu offers a more affordable, general-purpose model that can be easily attuned to company-specific needs. This dynamic reinforces the centrality of Big Tech in AI diffusion: large-scale generalist models lower adoption barriers for businesses but also concentrate control over the broader tech ecosystem. As more firms integrate the same AI models, feedback loops and platform-like network effects generate more data and opportunities to finetune the underlying algorithms, which in turn improves model performance and overall appeal.

Cross-sector integration extends beyond geographic and jurisdictional borders as companies pursue business opportunities in regions with legislative and fiscal incentives, innovative startups or skilled workforces. This can happen through mergers and acquisitions, investments, or by expanding with subsidiaries outside companies' home markets. Alphabet bolstered its AI toolkit by acquiring the UK-based DeepMind and Mandiant, a cybersecurity firm also offering AI consulting. SoftBank, the Japanese investment firm, finances AI startups across the US, Europe and Asia through its Vision Fund, whereas SAP, the German enterprise software leader, has set up innovation hubs for AI research and development in countries like Romania and Singapore. These corporate strategies allow companies already strong in certain sectors to establish footholds in new areas, diversifying their service offerings and revenue. Often, such cross-border integration reinforces existing corporate and regional hierarchies rather than upsetting them, a dynamic we also identify within sectors, as laid out below.

If left unchallenged by public authorities, cross-sectoral integration can thwart competition, as smaller regional players struggle to maintain their position. European cloud providers exemplify this dynamic. Cloud services consumption in Europe has grown consistently but the market share of European cloud providers has dropped to just 13 per cent. In the meantime, the three US hyperscalers (Amazon, Microsoft and Alphabet) control nearly three quarters of the global cloud market as of 2024.[41] These firms commonly integrate their cloud offerings with other digital products (AI-as-a-service in the case of Amazon; operating systems and productivity software for Microsoft). European firms' market share has declined because they lack the deep pockets of their American competitors. The latter can simply expand more quickly, offer lower prices, and provide more customized tech solutions. In consequence, European providers have retreated to serve regional customers with specific data needs or become appendices to US cloud giants.[42]

Without regulatory intervention, such as funding public alternatives or blocking corporate acquisitions, market dynamics ultimately limit consumer choice and leave businesses wanting to adopt AI systems overly dependent on dominant companies. In response, "digital sovereignty" initiatives have gathered steam especially since the more aggressive digital policies of the second Trump administration. We will return to their prospects for success in Chapter 7.

New hierarchies within sectors?

In contrast to business literature celebrating AI's benefits across the economy, AI diffusion will not let all firms in a sector thrive. Some will win as others lose. Neither does diffusion rejig the entire global economy along novel, non-capitalist trajectories, as theorists of techno-feudalism propose.[43] Instead, it largely reinforces existing hierarchies – both within industries and across countries and regions – even as it creates opportunities for highly adaptive firms. We should expect further consolidation among dominant market players combined with intensifying competition at the bottom, squeezing mid-tier companies.[44] Should AI indeed prove to be a transformative general-purpose technology, existing disparities would grow. AI-driven firms would secure first-mover advantages, capturing the lion's share of profits while late entrants chase increasingly squeezed margins.

In 2020, a consultancy report already warned of "a wider divide between AI leaders and the majority of companies still struggling to capitalize in the technology".[45] The outlook for AI-driven cost reduction was even less impressive, with only a third of businesses achieving usually modest efficiencies of below 10 per cent. Among firms that did benefit, only a small minority reported substantial gains, such as cost reductions over 20 per cent or revenue increases above 10 per cent. Corporate benefits from AI are clearly spread unevenly. Of course, AI diffusion is still in its early days, and firms continue searching for applications that generate long-term value. Many AI pilot projects either fail to scale or result in early losses. AI-driven income growth might yet pick up. Even then, however, these initial disparities risk hardening into lasting divides, as first movers secure competitive advantages that are difficult for laggards to replicate. So, what sets sectoral leaders apart in AI implementation?

A 2024 BCG report notes that top-performing firms use AITs not only for cost savings but also to drive revenue growth, integrating them across core operations and support functions like human resources or IT.[46] Additionally, they prioritize a few high-impact AI initiatives to scale effectively and to which they dedicate a larger share of their workforce. Reflecting the broader AI adoption trends discussed above, the highest concentration of "AI leaders" is found in sectors that are already well digitized, such as finance and software development.

This does not mean that the only AI beneficiaries are hyperscalers or highly digitized firms. Over half of "AI leaders" are traditional incumbents within their industries that have "strengthened their capabilities and are using them to build differentiated competitive advantages".[47] But smaller firms can benefit from AI if they can leverage their greater flexibility, strong leadership, partnerships with public research institutes and the absence of legacy tech constraints[48] which can provide a smoother path to AI adoption and the chance to outpace more established competitors.

For AI-driven gains to be shared broadly, two kinds of public interventions seem crucial: preventing dominant firms from absorbing emerging challengers and supporting small and medium-sized enterprises in keeping pace with AI adoption. Market incumbents are typically well-positioned to become early AI adopters and thus to solidify their dominance. These companies can leverage historically accumulated data and processing power across new AI-driven products and business lines. In the case of Amazon, its inventory forecasting and route optimization models reduce costs and improve delivery efficiency, a benchmark that competitors struggle to match. In retail, personalized recommender systems and dynamic pricing boost customer engagement and sales. And its cloud business offers high-end AI tools and platforms to third parties. Dominance generates resources (such as data, capital and computing power) that, when coupled with AITs, reinforce incumbents' market power.

The resources a firm already has at its disposal thus play a key role. Leading firms often attract the most highly qualified workers and operate with higher profit margins than their competitors.[49] Both factors are essential to developing and integrating resource-intensive AITs more effectively. In comparison, firms lacking financial capacity, or those dependent on external sources for data, skilled personnel, tech capacity or wholesale AITs, struggle to fully realize AI's benefits. Reality is thus very different from a scenario in which all companies in a sector gain access to a new technology simultaneously and on equal terms. Some forms of AI adoption may not require huge investments, especially when the technologies become commoditized and traded as off-the-shelf solutions. But even then, dominant firms have more resources to identify what makes most sense in economic terms.

Relatively high AI adoption rates are also found in smaller, younger firms like startups.[50] How can that be squared with the dynamic we just described? Limited resources often constrain their ability to invest in costly infrastructure, or the tech expertise required to leverage AITs. Output inaccuracies, biased data, and legal and security risks further complicate adoption, even if the height of these hurdles varies across industries and applications. Yet, among those firms experimenting with AI, its general-purpose capabilities make it an attractive cost-cutting tool across diverse tasks, particularly in marketing or recording financial transactions.

With cloud-based software-as-a-service models, smaller firms can integrate AI without hefty upfront costs or in-house development. The absence of legacy tech systems or bureaucratic complexities also smoothens adoption. We obviously have no data on AI's long-term benefits for small or young firms as yet. Indeed, AI adoption might yet boost competition and drive higher failure rates among small businesses. Either way, it cements the market positions of the companies that supply the AI and ancillary hardware and services. And where specific AI applications require advanced computing resources, disparate starting points between large incumbents, small or new firms and the rest of the market are exacerbated by the concentration of access to high-performing hardware now emerging as a bottleneck for firms seeking to develop proprietary AITs.

AI leaders' strategic positions can extract value from dependent businesses. This mirrors other global value chains, such as natural resource extraction, apparel or agriculture. The key to value appropriation lies in monopolizing an essential link in the chain while increasing competition in others. For instance, smallholders might be played off against each other to depress prices, all to the benefit of an agrifood behemoth. AITs offer similar potential. Computer vision models rely on enormous volumes of labelled visual data for applications like autonomous vehicles and facial recognition. This labelling work is typically outsourced via gig platforms, on which freelancers from regions with varying living costs compete for increasingly poorly paid tasks (we return to this dynamic in Chapter 5). By minimizing labour costs through outsourcing, AI adopters maximize value appropriation.

Where access to AITs determines business success, AI vendors can charge steep prices as tech gatekeepers, certainly if they face little competition. Consider the "algorithmic attention rents" earned by advertising platforms like Google and Facebook through the monetization of user data to third parties in an increasingly oligopolistic online ad market.[51] As advertisers flock to them, their economies of scale boost profit margins, reminiscent of extractive practices in finance and real estate. Across these sectors, firms generate high returns not necessarily by producing more or better products, but by controlling access to scarce valuable resources (information, capital or land) and extracting value through rents rather than productive investment.

These practices have traditionally evaded antitrust enforcement, as tech giants operate across multiple markets without fully dominating any. On top of this, many of their consumer-facing products (Google Search or Facebook Messenger) are technically free to consumers, making it hard for antitrust legislators to argue that companies abuse their pricing power. Such patterns of dominance highlight the need to rethink what is called the economic approach to antitrust law, as happened during Lina Khan's tenure as FTC chair. But even when antitrust cases emerge – such as the US Department of Justice's lawsuit against Google for monopolizing search and advertising – cases can drag on for years, or risk becoming mired in political battles that dilute their impact.

Will production-relevant AITs be developed, owned and freely sold by standalone companies in the AI sector, making them available to other industries? Or will AI adopters seek exclusive access to such services either by acquiring AI firms or building in-house systems? For example, ServiceNow works with partners in target countries which then market, resell, consult on and implement tailor-made versions of its AI-powered workflow management systems. In Europe, intermediaries with local ICT expertise such as the French Orange, German T-Systems or Swisscom build and consult on customized licenses on behalf of big US-based software-as-a-service platforms. Preliminary evidence suggests that AI-adopting companies go for a mix of off-the-shelf solutions and significantly customized models or solutions developed entirely in-house, with sectors such as energy and technology favouring customization and in-house development more heavily than business, legal and professional services.[52]

Much like the decision to use cloud services over building proprietary tech, firms may choose generic AITs for lower costs, faster deployment and lower expertise requirements, even if that means potential vendor lock-in. For example, rather than developing its own customer verification model, a small bank might use Onfido for identity checks while checking account sign-ups. Conversely, larger firms with deeper pockets may opt for highly customized or in-house AI solutions, prioritizing tailored functionality or the opportunity to resell these technologies as on-demand services. Additionally, companies handling very sensitive data (such as in clinical trials) or operating in stricter privacy law contexts are more likely to develop AITs internally, even if this comes with higher costs or longer development timelines.

How readily AITs will be available to companies in a sector is partly also a question of public policy and regulation. States and regional blocs might force firms to share key innovations to curb monopolistic structures. Avenues include broader access to AITs through open source projects, public data repositories or financial incentives for AI experimentation. However, even when such efforts materialize, like France's Andromède sovereign cloud project, they may still be coopted by dominant industry players or struggle to match the quality of established private alternatives. National strategies to build local tech infrastructure and diversifying economies such as Kuwait's Vision 2035 or the

Qatari Digital Agenda 2030 aspire to strengthen domestic firms in the digital ecosystem. But in practice, they frequently involve partnerships with hyperscalers to gain access to advanced tech and expertise.

Indeed, vertical integration – a business controlling upstream or downstream stages of its supply chain – has long been an antitrust concern. In the post-ChatGPT AI boom, trustbusters in the US, EU and UK have probed partnerships between tech giants and AI startups, such as Microsoft's deal with OpenAI or Amazon and Alphabet's billions poured into rival startup Anthropic. The aim is to prevent market dominance in one sector from spilling over into another, in this case big cloud providers integrating vertically into AI development.

But there are limits to public authorities' incentives or ability to counter such dynamics through binding policies. In a "national champions" strategy, dominance in domestic markets can be a price to pay for firms' successful international expansion, a tension that has bedevilled EU competition policy for decades, as strict enforcement has obstructed potential European champions in global corporate competition. Politically, strong enforcement is easier when companies are foreign and less domestic employment is at stake. At the same time, foreign companies may enjoy political backing from their home governments, as in the US, complicating the political calculation of how heavy-handedly to enforce competition policy.

Only governments with deep pockets, strong digital infrastructure and economically significant markets can afford to push back against the business models of sectoral leaders. Economic resources allow states to invest in regulatory enforcement, fund public alternatives or absorb the fallout of pushing for stricter rules, whereas dependable infrastructures are key to developing domestic AI capabilities that reduce reliance on dominant firms. But even when state-level interventions are enacted, success remains uncertain. The EU AI Act's requirements, for instance, led OpenAI, Meta and Apple to delay releasing their latest AITs in Europe, citing "legal uncertainty".[53] Even in major digital economies, powerful firms can leverage the threat of withholding advanced technologies to pressure policymakers into watering down legislation or offering special treatment.

Governments' narrow economistic focus on promoting domestic AI champions for global competitiveness feeds debates about digital sovereignty, in which the geopolitical and economic pressures of the putative AI race lead to zero-sum confrontational strategies for AI diffusion.[54] The EU's push for digital sovereignty is a case in point, even if it remains an open question whether the bloc can wean itself off dependence on American technology. This techno-determinist, nation-first and big business approach can hinder global cooperation on distributing AI's benefits more widely or aligning its progress with human rights and worker protection. It also clashes with a more pluralistic model of AI governance – one where citizens, regardless of their country's technological or economic standing, can have their say on how critical technologies are built. To illuminate the wider ripple effects of AITs beyond product markets, we turn to labour markets and less prosperous world regions in the next two chapters.

5

Uneven effects on labour

AI's effect on the world of work is not a new worry, tapping into a time-honoured angst of tech-driven job destruction. In the broader frame of labour and technological evolution, it is but the latest chapter in a fraught and contested history spanning centuries. To be sure, optimism reigned early in the twentieth century. John Maynard Keynes had mused about the *Economic Possibilities for Our Grandchildren*, foreseeing that productivity increases would reduce work to a few hours each day, leaving ample time for leisure. Real-world tech progress has defied that prediction. Even affluent workers seem to be as stressed out as ever, and while working hours have reduced in many advanced economies (particularly in the EU) they did not do so as dramatically as Keynes envisaged.[1] The sanguine view that automation would teleport us into a world of endless procrastination has only survived as a tongue-in-cheek caricature of genuine utopia.[2]

Considering what is at stake, the debate among economists is surprisingly narrow. So rather than just rehashing job loss predictions, we zoom out for a more holistic understanding of AI's impact on labour. We offer three shifts in perspective. First, much discussion in this area follows the hype-versus-doom thread in trying to pinpoint where exactly jobs might be lost or augmented through ever more capable automation. This debate deserves revisiting. The job-altering or job-destroying forces vary enormously across sectors. And they play out differently in different places depending on local economic profiles, wealth levels, policy priorities and labour market institutions. AITs' impact on jobs depends on political variables as much as on economic or technological ones.

Second, the obsession with predicting AI-related job losses and augmentation dynamics reduces "human labour" to a mere factor of production, or a "fictitious commodity" in the Polanyian sense. Automation apparently operates in isolation from socio-political relations, steered by an invisible hand in response to wages levels. Labourers – the actual people – are accorded little agency. We conceptualize labour as a social relation shaped by government interventions (think labour laws) but also by dominant narratives and the value and meaning that is attributed to human toil. These considerations pick up Chapter 4's conceptual thread about how "AI-driven productivity" is socially constructed.

Third, political context and meaning-making also matter for AI as a tool to structure or monitor human labour. Through live performance tracking, nudging and disciplining, AI substantially transforms labour relations beyond mere automation: it decreases workers' autonomy, estranges them from social relations in the workplace and redistributes power to management. This dimension gets lost in the narrow focus on job losses. AI-related monitoring and control happens inside of companies, in arm's length relationships and when work is intermediated through online platforms such as Uber, Meituan or Delivery Hero. Why do we see these dynamics unfolding? How do they fit into well-worn patterns of struggle between capital and labour? And how do geography and politics affect when, where and how AI is used to control work and workers in these ways?

Lost jobs, different jobs, new jobs, better jobs?

Economists have offered wildly different estimates of tech-related job market upheaval.[3] Most of these focus on countries in which technologies have diffused substantially already, effectively the Global North, which makes it a natural starting point for our investigations. Important labour market effects elsewhere reflect asymmetrical global power relations: mining for rare earths in the Global South, for example, is primarily driven by tech demand in richer countries (including for things like electric vehicle batteries), just as online gig work in countries such as Kenya or the Philippines thrives on changing business models of multinationals in the Global North. For now, we largely follow the Global North focus of the academic debate and return to the global dynamics in Chapter 6.

In a paper published in 2013 that jumpstarted much of the wider discussion, Frey and Osborne identified 47 per cent of US jobs as "highly susceptible to computerization" within a decade or two.[4] To many, that prediction was as spectacular as it was erroneous. Arntz and colleagues considered only 9 per cent of US jobs at risk; Nedelkoska and Quintini 14 per cent.[5] Assessments differed in other respects, too. Some expected workers on the bottom rungs of the labour market ladder to be hit hardest, whereas others feared a hollowing-out of the middle segment. And as tech itself evolved, predictions also shifted. As will become clear, we are sceptical about narrowly quantitative predictions of the labour market impact of AITs, as much as we understand the temptation to offer them. The phenomenon is too complex, varied and contingent. That said, the debate has much to offer as an object of inquiry about the dynamics at play here.

Labour shortages in rich countries have boosted interest in worker-replacing technologies. Especially since the Covid pandemic, many sectors have struggled to fill vacancies. The retiring baby boomer generation withdraws workers from labour markets while also placing increasing demands on the care sector and pension funds. Birthrates across rich countries have been below replacement rates for decades, so that without inward migration, the working population has been falling. At the same time, demographic pressures vary widely across the globe. Some countries contend with people ageing out of jobs, others with many new labour market entrants, and some face both issues. Labour market conditions also bear the imprint of government policies on female employment, childcare options, retraining and migration. Nevertheless, for employers who struggle to find workers with the skill profiles they seek it makes sense to respond by trying to increase productivity through automation.

The attractiveness of automation varies with wage rates: a robot or new IT system has more appeal where workers are more expensive. This dynamic not only helps explain the chequered automation landscape, but it can also be self-reinforcing. Countries on the path of digitization and automation have incentives to create the requisite infrastructure, from 5G connectivity to educational systems that emphasize digital skills. Once this infrastructure is established, additional steps towards digital automation become less costly. And if at least some of the fruits of automation are shared with workers themselves, real wages rise further, incentivizing yet more automation. In other words, where people earn little money, there may be less incentive to automate, and low levels of automation also keep real wages low. Both dynamics together create a self-reinforcing pattern of automation or non-automation.

Beyond these wage-related impacts on labour markets, economists divide the effects of AI into two categories: full automation-substitution on the one hand and augmentation on the other. A common starting point is the question whether AITs replace or complement jobs. In our opinion, they can clearly do both. Sometimes, AITs simply take over jobs as they are, such as reading and assessing insurance claims or sorting mail. In other instances, new things become possible with AI (extracting shell gas from previously untapped reservoirs), but people remain essential. Some jobs simply disappear, some hardly change, some remain but have AI integrated into them, and some are radically transformed or even totally new.

Augmentation is not always better news for workers than replacement. Much depends on how companies use the saved labour costs, productivity gains and potentially rising demand for cheaper products. Where AITs do not replace human labour in its entirety, they can be introduced either to make workers more productive (enabling them to do more in less time) or more exchangeable (with AITs taking over tasks that would require intense human training, meaning that they homogenize and standardize skills that people need to do a particular job). Navigation systems mean that taxi drivers no longer have to memorize city maps. Reducing such knowledge barriers may also make jobs more accessible. Skill shortages, in other words, can be tackled by simplifying jobs. And even where AI does not address acute shortages, it lowers entry barriers, increases competition for such jobs and thereby depresses wage rates.

The WEF's Future of Jobs survey among employers illustrates differences across sectors. Companies in insurance and pension management and electronics emphasize outright automation of processes and tasks; sectors such as medical services or accommodation, food and leisure put more weight on complementing and augmenting the workforce through AITs.[6] Despite this, in all the sectors surveyed, at least 45 per cent of employers said they wanted to use new technologies (not only AITs) to complement workers, and no less than 55 per cent wanted to automate. Companies clearly do both.

In theory, then, productivity increases through automation should mean that production costs decrease. If that translates into falling prices, demand may rise, and the net employment effect may be neutral or even positive. A sector may expand as the prices of its outputs fall. Of course, such price elasticity in demand varies significantly across products and demographic groups. How automation affects labour markets is therefore impossible to predict at this level of generality. If taxis in Amsterdam were a lot cheaper than they are now, people would use them more often. Would Amsterdammers also buy more bikes if they cost half as much? We doubt it, given that just about everyone has one already. This exposes the limits of current debates: even if we could predict how easy it is to automate (part of) a job with an econometric function, that would say little about the aggregate labour market effect of such automation (even before exploring major intervenors such as political institutions).

One prominent strand of the debate has tried to figure out which workers would be hit hardest by AITs, and whether, in consequence, we should expect labour markets to fragment further into good, well-paying jobs at the top and precarious employment or even full replacement at the bottom. The point of departure for this debate was the twentieth-century experience: after machinery had first made production in factories possible, further advances eventually obliterated more jobs than they created.[7] Factory jobs for people with manual skills dwindled, paralleling job losses in agriculture as labour-saving technology spread across the sector. Technological progress, so the idea went, punished people at the bottom end of labour markets especially, as they were the easiest to replace.

AITs have shaken that conventional wisdom. Frey and Osborne's early study had identified three bottlenecks: tasks that require high physical mobility and dexterity, those where creative intelligence is needed, and those with a heavy social component are hard to automate.[8] The authors focused on digital technologies preceding most AITs, but the implication remains important today: the skills highlighted as "hard to automate" cut across wage categories. High physical mobility and dexterity, for example, are key for people who work around other humans (nurses or surgeons, for example) or in and around houses – cleaners, plumbers, roofers and so on. In contrast, a lot of easy-to-automate jobs are routine service work, often behind keyboards and computer screens: salary administration, travel planning or insurance. Assembly line workers and truck drivers scored dangerously high on automation risk. Even though the occupations varied significantly and cut across the wage spectrum, Frey and Osborne still expected "computerisation [to be] principally confined to low-skill and low-wage occupations".[9] Such a dynamic would further feed labour market dualization, which has been going on for quite some time already.

If a share of the population sees its incomes swell, and those in lower labour market segments see precarity rising and earning opportunities falling, the latter group may increasingly find itself serving the former. In consequence, one fast-expanding sector in the dualization phase is that of personal or outsourced services: everything from nail studios to food delivery. A growing group of workers will satisfy the wants of people whose incomes are more directly tied to where profits accrue – wants related to travel, housing, luxury goods, casual consumption, and so on. Such stratification is not new, but it is amplified by the wealth appropriation capacities that AI creates, and it is reminiscent of previous ages with unequal socio-economic relations.[10]

But dynamics can be complicated. As mentioned, the arrival of autonomous vehicles used to inspire fears that truck drivers would soon all be out of a job. Now, the WEF's Future of Jobs report, based on employer surveys, has "Light Truck and Delivery Services Drivers" as the second-largest *growing* job category.[11] In the form of e-commerce and concomitant parcel delivery, digital technologies are once more the driver, but now in a direction diametrically opposed to earlier expectations. This shows just how much of a guessing game this is. And still, the specificity of economists' headline-grabbing predictions remains emblematic of their over-confidence in modelling these impacts.

Recent evidence complicates the picture of deepening AI-driven labour market dualization. Much of that shift comes from generative AI capturing employers' (and economists') attention. These innovations allow people to do work previously reserved for those with much higher levels of education or experience.[12] Here, it is the highly skilled whose skill premiums shrivel. The labour market impact of generative AI is very different to that of an algorithm streamlining operations in a warehouse.

Consider a few examples: relatively inexperienced lawyers can leverage AI to sift through thousands of court cases to find the right precedents; inexperienced web designers can use AI to generate the graphics and website structure; inexperienced coders can ask GitHub Copilot for bug fixes.[13] As LLM performance improves, it may be people who hitherto considered their jobs safe who are hit next. Hui and colleagues, for example, found that generative AI not only dented the volume and remuneration of creative work offered to freelancers overall, the effect was also more pronounced for the strongest performers.[14] The latter do not thrive or survive but instead find themselves more exposed to second-rate competition than before. At the same time, superstars seem to be immune to full replacement for now. Artists with clout like Scarlett Johansson or Taylor Swift have enough of a personal brand and fans to be irreplaceable. The hollowing-out happens below the threshold of personal fame and reputation.

The net effects of automation are even harder to measure, let alone predict. Yes, some poorly-remunerated jobs may disappear – a dynamic that we find more in relatively rich countries than in less affluent ones.[15] At the same time, we have seen labour demand in that segment increase in the US, potentially because tasks supported with AI become accessible to people previously unable to perform them due to a lack of training.[16] And as if the picture was not muddled enough already, observers also reach different conclusions because they mean different things when they talk about AI. Trying to estimate labour market effects with logistics and process optimization capabilities in mind leads to very different conclusions than a focus on generative AI.

And AI also creates jobs: programmers, workers who create content through competent prompting of generative AI models, people building and maintaining the requisite hardware, and so on. Demand for people with AI-relevant computer skills has risen sharply. This effect is real and meaningful even for very recent AI advances: as of 2024, roughly 0.2 per cent of job postings in countries like the UK, the US, France and Germany mentioned "GenAI".[17] However, future job creation is even less predictable than AI's effects on existing jobs. Companies' need for new skills, as AI tools enter their offices, could be rather abrupt. And new skillsets may themselves end up in the crosshairs of automation before long. For example, becoming a prompt engineer appeared to be a promising career prospect in 2024, because coaxing high-quality images or videos out of DALL-E or Sora was trickier than it first seemed. But as additional AI models have been built to smooth interactions with generative AI, effective prompting may become much less of a specialist skill. The demands of and for AI are anyone's guess, and AI itself may quickly replace or downgrade the jobs currently required to build it.

The next two waves of AITs – agentic AI and AI-cum-robotics – will have their own labour market effects. Agentic AI in essence refers to systems that can execute (normally digital) tasks autonomously. Common examples include booking train tickets or sending emails with standardized messages (imagine asking your phone to tell someone you will be half an hour late). Agentic AI appears to be the next phase in automating office-based work, reinforcing dynamics already set in motion by LLMs. But when tech companies showcase agentic AI, they commonly portray people organizing their private life differently: scheduling doctor appointments, ordering pizza, and so on. At least for now, that does not strike us like a "gamechanger" as the advertised uses remain conspicuously limited and for now humans still need to double-check what the agents have done.

Advances in robotics are different. AI can add sensitivity to surroundings (computer vision and smart sensors), and it can use learning techniques to create adaptable policies (effectively instructions) for robots. Often, AI-powered robots are trained by humans first, who perform particular motions with the robot arms, like marionettes, such that the robot "learns" them. Reinforcement learning is then used to let the robot know whether something worked or not. With AI added to robots, we can automate tasks that require adaptability and dexterity – previously beyond their reach. There is thus another automation wave on the horizon: robotics 2.0, not pre-programmed but learning on the job. These technologies are harder to scale because new hardware is necessary for every instance and because robots may need context-specific training (working in a particular factory), which is a clear difference from general-purpose AI like LLMs. For the time being, there is a limit to how cheap robots will become, and poorly paid humans may still be cheaper than automation.

That said, once skills can be generalized and transferred from one robot to another through a kind of general robotic language, with the right hardware in place, there might be much more automation coming our way than the current focus on generative AI admits. And that trend is not exclusive to the Global North. Once we disaggregate the data from the *Future of Jobs* survey across regions, it is evident that in Sub-Saharan Africa, for example, five out of six employers say that AI and information processing technologies will be drivers of transformation in their organizations. And they expect the impact of robots and autonomous systems to hit Southeast Asia the hardest, with a lot of local manufacturing susceptible to robotization. The opposite is true for Central Asia, the Middle East and Northern and Sub-Saharan Africa, where there is relatively little manufacturing. The richest countries globally fall between these two groups.

While some global comparisons exist, most statistics and discussions skew heavily towards the roughly one billion people living in rich countries, ignoring the fact that they are a minority of the global population. Statistics about "jobs" and "employers" also gloss over that labour markets are often highly informal (including for the data annotation work that fuels AI models). A large chunk of the global population does not have "jobs" in the way people in affluent countries imagine them, with a clear contract and monthly pay. The impact AI has on their livelihoods certainly cannot be gleaned from reports like WEF's. We lack up-to-date data for systematic answers ourselves and so must stick with what is available. It should be clear, however, that the widespread indifference humanity has shown to its weakest members does not bode well for how the potential benefits of AI will be shared – or not.

Beyond aggregate job gains or losses, AI diffusion means that many people will now need different skills than before. Traditional skills lose value, for example the ability to do maths in your head or being able to write without grammatical errors. Others become more important: social skills (empathy, leadership), IT-related skills (prominently including AI and big data) and critical and analytical faculties.[18] Lifelong learning, too, features high on the list. What employers look for changes quickly, and that includes skills that are not learned in a day or two, in contrast to operating a straightforward machine. Skill mismatches are clearly a problem as labour demand changes.

A lot of knowledge work has now become data analysis work. Marketing, for example, has turned into sifting through large amounts of customer data. The same will be true for weather prediction, but also tasks connected to running infrastructure, jobs in finance, and everything that has moved from the real world into apps: booking travel, sharing information with citizens, administering reimbursements from insurance companies, making and selling music and other creative content, publishing, corporate communication and retail. We need drastically fewer of the people who used to work in these sectors and more data scientists and IT specialists. AI will only intensify that trend.

For the political-economic impact of this dynamic, the speed of change is crucial. It is not new that tech change boosts demand for some skills and workers and dampens it for others. But it may be impossible to train and retrain people in sync with the rapid transformation, with those thrown out of their old jobs unable to do the new ones. Labour market dislocation inevitably follows. "Demand for labour" often sounds as if people are completely fungible. But they most certainly are not, and nor should they be.

Where workers are mobile across borders (such as in the EU) these labour market disruptions can exacerbate shortages. Many young and highly skilled people from Central and Eastern Europe, for example, find work in other EU member states, leaving their home countries with acute skills gaps.[19] To the degree that the demand for new skill profiles is widespread, we should expect further specialization and differentiation of countries' economic profiles because sought-after workers vote with their feet, exposing their home countries to brain and skills drain.

What about companies that directly develop AITs themselves? Where should we expect that job creation to appear, both directly and indirectly (the accompanying office cleaners, canteen workers, and so on)? Tech jobs are clustered, most famously in Silicon Valley. As Annalee Saxenian has chronicled, the Bay Area offered propitious conditions for the agglomeration of IT firms, even compared to promising competitors such as the ecosystem that had built up around the Massachusetts Institute of Technology in the Boston Area.[20]

Once such clusters are in place, they attract more companies. Recently, many European firms ready to expand in AI shifted their attention to the US, claiming that is simply where the action is. Mistral opened a large office there; Pathway, also French, moved its HQ to the US altogether. Other companies like the Finnish SiloAI were also drawn closer into the American AI ecosystem when it was acquired by Advanced Micro Devices (AMD) in 2024. A self-reinforcing dynamic follows: workers go where the companies are, but companies also go where they find the workers. As EU politicians clamouring for greater European sovereignty in AI have discovered, counteracting that dynamic is hard. It requires not only fostering a pool of homegrown experts but also spawning local clusters of firms strong enough to keep them there. After all, the latent mobility of IT experts (and AI experts in particular) is high. Workers perceive this field, and the companies that operate in it, less and less as segmented along national lines, but as an integrated transnational space of elite tech work.[21]

In the first instance, "new jobs created by AI" conjures up an image of someone hacking away at a keyboard in an open office loft. There is a completely different facet, however, when the diffusion of AI boosts the demand for hardware and the raw materials required to power resource-hungry algorithms. Many people labour out of the limelight to make the seemingly virtual AI products work.[22] That includes those who collect, collate or clean the data that is used for training AI models. It also includes propping up products that are presented to us as digital (say, self-driving cars or chatbots) but that do actually require human guidance behind the scenes. An early *Time* magazine investigation revealed that to finetune ChatGPT via reinforcement learning from human feedback, OpenAI contracted Global South workers for meagre wages to sift through large volumes of harmful content, exposing them to the often-disturbing online material contained in the chatbot's training data.[23] Also geographically, much of this work is far removed from the shiny offices in which we normally think AI is made. We will return to this key feature of globally asymmetric resource extraction and value generation processes in Chapter 6.

How narratives and institutions shape AI's impact on labour

The early focus in AI research on machines imitating human intelligence was to prove consequential for how interactions between AITs and labour are discussed today. Taking humans as the measure of what machines could and should do revealed an anthropocentric arrogance, ignoring forms of intelligence or competence different from ours, for example recognizing wavelengths of sound or light that humans cannot. The anthropomorphized ghost of AI waiting to replace or augment human labour haunts us in another way, too: it feeds techno-solutionist narratives in which labour can be ever more optimized and squeezed as a cost factor. Such labour optimization desires were baked into AI development from day one; Herbert Simon already dreamt of machines replacing biased and costly public sector workers during the famous 1956 Dartmouth gathering.[24]

Do AI systems live up to hopes of less biased, more precise and cost-efficient task completion? Journals and tech blogs are replete with examples of mediocre AI decisions and outputs, for example when the new AI-generated Duolingo quizzes – a previous selling point for the language-learning app – are less funny, boringly predictable and more often factually wrong than those previously created by the 100 translators whose contracts had already been terminated.[25]

Importantly for us as political economists, the narrow economistic framing of AITs and labour productivity – irrespective of whether AI can actually get the job done – misrepresents (labour) markets as unrelated to political institutions. How societies construe "labour" in automation and augmentation waves – as a mere factor of production or as a contingent social relation – is not merely philosophical. Where governments stand on this can decide how well people are protected against the most adverse consequences of AI-driven automation. It shapes whether firms are allowed to externalize the occupational health costs of production onto others (often, the public purse or countries far away from the shiny headquarters of AI-first firms), and how potential productivity gains are shared. Do AITs feed a survival-of-the-fittest spiral in which the least productive are replaced, or do the fruits of innovation get shared to cushion adverse societal effects?

When economists or politicians ask if AITs replace or complement workers, the assumption is that complementarity is preferable because it stabilizes demand for human labour, which becomes more productive. To our mind, that offers little solace: yes, we may still need some humans in the office or on the shopfloor to get things done. But if we require only half as many as before because productivity has risen, that can only count as good news if the other half at least gets retraining, access to social benefits, or some universal income (again, many of these depend on political will and capacity).

A narrow focus on labour productivity also ignores the deeper value and complexity of many jobs, particularly those involving human connection. As Alison Pugh shows in *The Last Human Job*, roles like teachers, nurses, police officers and therapists involve more than just delivering a service; they require what she calls "connective labour", the emotional and interpersonal work that adds meaning and worth.[26] A teacher is not merely a conduit for knowledge but also a motivator and source of warmth, helping students strive as learners and human beings. Nurses do more than administer care: they offer comfort, hope, and companionship to patients in challenging times. Even random conversations between police officers and shop owners during neighbourhood patrols are not distractions or embellishments but integral to building trust. A myopic view of labour fails to recognize these elements, feeding flawed optimism about automation.

While algorithms may streamline workflows by refining the division of labour, they also eliminate organizational slack and reduce opportunities for serendipitous problem-solving.[27] Tasks become increasingly fragmented, and most workers may never see the bigger picture of a project or interact with their colleagues beyond their narrowly defined roles, whether putting together a grant application or designing a house. Even from a strict productivity perspective, something essential may be lost: the personal interactions we typically take for granted. Currently, we frequently encounter service workers with only a superficial understanding of their roles. A skilled hotel receptionist, in contrast, does far more than process payments and hand out keycards. They have the knowledge, experience and the discretion to help us with all manner of specific requests and questions. Standardized and algorithmic workflows end up deskilling humans, making it easier to rotate workers in and out of roles with minimal retraining. As AI-driven automation furthers the commodification of labour, aspects of work that resist this dynamic – often because they are hard to quantify, to make visible or to standardize – are increasingly sidelined. Tacit knowledge, the de facto glue of many processes, risks being overlooked and undervalued.

Karl Polanyi's 1944 book *The Great Transformation*, with the first industrial revolution in England in mind, rings true to us as we consider today's

AI transformation: "[a] belief in spontaneous progress must make us blind to the role of government in economic life".[28] The warning that Polanyi sends to the present state of labour is clear: if governments leave answers to social questions to self-regulating markets, productivity booms and wealth generated with AITs may co-exist with large-scale deprivation, joblessness, or simply a rise of impoverished working conditions. And the failure to embed market dynamics in social institutions and combat disintegration may propel the rise of fascism, national protectionism, geopolitical rivalry and war, just as it did in the early twentieth century.

Institutions matter in at least two ways in this reading. First, as initial inaugurators of markets – that is before they can even be treated as "free" markets – which protect property owners and enable the extraction of value from "fictitious" commodities that are not naturally made for sale, such as land, labour, money and now also user data.[29] And second, as bulwarks against adverse consequences of unrestrained market economies: excessive unemployment, poverty, labour deprivation and related waves of social unrest. That AITs find their way into the world of work largely as profit maximizing tools to replace or augment labour does not flow from the inherent properties of the technologies themselves. It is a function of the socio-economic conditions in which they flourish, stabilized by institutions such as intellectual property or labour law, trade regimes, antitrust policy and taxation regimes.

The economistic calculation that more AI equals higher labour productivity ignores the heavy (and completely new) data annotation labour that underpins models' growing accuracy, scale and complexity. This, too, is a matter of regulatory leniency enabling market exchanges and global divisions of labour to operate *as if* human labour were a mere commodity. As long as precarious gig workers in Venezuela or graduate interns in China are paid a pittance to turn masses of frequently disturbing content into "clean" and correctly labelled data, the productivity-positive calculation may superficially hold.[30] But if corporate responsibility were enforced across the AI stack, if fair wages were paid for data annotation, or if the costs for mental health treatments after job-related exposure to disturbing content were factored into the production costs of AI systems, the productivity calculation would look much less rosy.

Jobs in the rich world are not necessarily "replaced" by a machine in a free market; they are frequently morphed into AI jobs in other parts of the world in which economic dependencies and weak institutions make workers more readily exploitable, a dynamic familiar from sectors like apparel or manufacturing. Considered in this way, "AI doesn't primarily destroy jobs, but redistributes them to poorly paid workers and unpaid consumers".[31] The growth and variety of models and datasets in different waves of AI "breakthroughs" predicated on "hidden labour" – most importantly in data annotation – is far removed from the unicorn labs.[32]

All this rhymes with the historical record. Past automation did not make labour obsolete, but it often shifted it to cheaper production sites. But automation did not automatically ease the burden on workers in the industrialized countries or create a much more equal division of the fruits of labour.[33] To achieve that, political pressure, largely driven by organized workers, remained essential.[34]

There is thus no automatism that translates rising labour productivity into higher compensation. This was Polanyi's initial puzzle, too: how could technological progress, unprecedented wealth accumulation and high productivity coincide with poverty and pauperism in England in the nineteenth and early twentieth century? The fantasy of a self-regulating market would devour society in a "satanic mill", Polanyi thought, unless it was contained by measures that reflect the inherently social nature of land, labour and money as forms of human exchange. Consider that productivity increases (including through automation) have outpaced compensation since the 1980s in the US and in Japan and since the 1990s in Europe.[35] And it is the owners of capital who have pocketed a disproportionate share of the benefits.[36]

What matters, then, is states' variable appetite and capacity for meaningful regulation of markets to redistribute risks and benefits and mitigate their most adverse societal effects. Welfare state arrangements in the late nineteenth and mid-twentieth century in some European countries count as the most advanced institutionalization of pushback against destructive capitalist dynamics. Citizens' relative dependence on market income (in return for paid labour, for most of us) was cushioned through publicly financed education and training. Universal labour law and minimum wages reduced exploitability in any one job.

As in the past, welfare, training and labour law institutions also matter for the relative impact of AI-driven automation on workers. Depending on the country or sector in which people work, they may enjoy legal protections, use publicly funded training to build up skills, or simply rely on a social safety net to dampen the effects of automation. It makes a difference whether a legal clerk or business analyst replaced by AITs falls immediately back into a residual safety net where means-testing devours any personal savings (as in the UK), whether she can maintain her living standard for a while with a moderate wage replacement rate and access retraining measures (for example, in the German combination of Bismarckian unemployment insurance with vocational training), or even has access to generous tax-funded social benefits (in Norway or Finland). In poorer countries where the welfare state has emerged relatively recently, the existence of a universal basic income (such as Brazil's *Bolsa Família*) also renders people less vulnerable to exploitation as cheap gig workers. In addition, regulatory measures such as the EU's 2024 Platform Work Directive aim to formalize at least some of the highly fragmented and exploitable labour relations in AI-driven gig work. They help gig workers access sick leave, holiday pay and training opportunities, even as they may push up the price of their labour and potentially dent demand for it.

A lot depends on workers' bargaining power and thus on unionization rates, relative support from parties in power (traditionally the social democrats), exposure to competitive pressures from open trade and capital markets, as well as labour market conditions. These factors typically swing free from technological development itself. From studies on platform worker protests we know that union involvement varies enormously across countries. In Europe, New Zealand and Australia, unions were lead actors in more than half of the protests studied.[37] Everywhere else, they had a similar role in one out of five protests at best, with informal worker groups being most prominent. And worker agency is not only a question of confronting employers or clients in gig work, but also of creatively navigating the work environment that gig work creates. Mohammed Anwar and Mark Graham have explored the resilience and reworking strategies of remote gig workers in Africa, evidencing the micro-strategies workers use to build alliances with other workers, exchange experiences, share work and circumvent restrictions established by clients in rich countries.[38]

Political-economic and geopolitical dynamics also influence where new AI jobs appear. Many IT clusters beyond the US thrived as returnees from Silicon Valley set up successful companies in their countries of origin. This dynamic diffuses US-style working cultures through the global tech sector. But it only materializes where conditions in the country of origin are conducive to setting up shop there, either because economic and political conditions are welcoming, or because the requisite infrastructure is in place. This dynamic is evident in Israel and India for example, but not in Iran or Central Asia, despite IT talents having moved from there to the US. The diffusion of AI know-how from Silicon Valley through return migrants is far from universal. In addition, the earlier wave of IT development that Saxenian studied (in the early 2000s) happened in a very different political climate from the one we observe now. Then, serious geopolitical competition seemed far off, and economic globalization felt like a one-way street. National security or competitiveness were relative non-issues because global hierarchies were unambiguous. At the same time, the common vision in those days was a "connected" world, in which tech hubs like Taipei, Bangalore, Singapore, Tel Aviv and others would span the globe like a high-tech net.

Fast-forward to the 2020s, and labour markets are quickly becoming more fragmented, especially as the barriers between China and the US have gone up. Silicon Valley was and remains attractive for Chinese tech workers, but the securitization of the digital sector (and of AITs in particular) has made it progressively harder for them to work there. Fragmentation is imposed from the top. As the second Trump administration promises a more aggressive digital policy, other countries or regions may also find themselves either in the cross-hairs of restrictive US policy or considering a higher emphasis on breeding and keeping talent at home. Moreover, inherently oligopolistic dynamics mean that among allied or cooperating countries, we should expect more pronounced hierarchies once again: top-level AI firms concentrated in the US, China, and maybe some European countries, with firms that are effectively subsidiaries to them elsewhere. As geopolitical tensions have returned with a vengeance, the vision of "networked globalization" has turned out to be an illusion.

Lots of conceivable AI innovation could in fact boost the demand for labour – if only someone paid for it.[39] Latent labour demand is massive, across the world. Consider the potential of AI systems that would shed light on individual students' learning styles and difficulties, which could then be the basis for much more targeted forms of individual tutoring by humans. AI could also help identify latent needs or create new ones altogether (such as preventative medicine or early interventions to address mental health problems). In such cases, AITs might point us to opportunities for using human labour to reach societal goals in education, public health, societal cohesion, and so on. If too few people are hired, or job conditions are not attractive enough, that says as much about insufficient redistribution or governments' unwillingness to invest in strong public services as it does about "demand" as a somehow isolated economic variable. To what degree AITs get used in ways that enhance societal welfare depends on political will and the availability of funds to bolster public services, if need be through redistribution. In most places, the current political climate mitigates against such a development.

A narrow, economistic perspective on labour as a factor of production to be replaced or optimized with AI misconceives what most people, including we as authors, experience and value as a deeply social and affective relation. Work can be a source of contentment or identification in life, or a source of discontent and alienation. It is an opportunity to connect with other people, simply as one human with the other or as potential allies in collective political struggles. In the public sector, labour is the human and, in the best case, empathetic face of an otherwise cold bureaucracy and the bearer of the discretionary power that can recognize an individual and their rights in an anonymous mass of data. In all these dimensions, we find, the diffusion of AI has serious ramifications.

In the public sector, for example, AI effects on workers could be handled in quite different ways. Currently, austerity and cost-saving paradigms are often the backdrop that makes AITs attractive in the first place. As in the production of cars or services for banking customers, AITs can make the distribution of public goods and services more cost-effective. This logic might not seem worthy of inquiry through an economic lens – is it not simply the public sector adapting (allegedly more rational) business logics of productivity gains? From a social constructivist perspective, it is neither obvious nor materially given but normalizes a selective and self-serving vision of how states should work (like businesses) and for what tech should be used (to cut wage expenditure and money distributed to people, for example as welfare state provisions). Some public administration scholars even fear that nothing short of a "technology-driven disruption" could render century-old government structures and processes "irrelevant in the near future".[40]

The current push for procuring AI in the public sector echoes a long-standing discussion about new public management among public administration scholars.[41] That has pitted visions of an active state – a human-centric provider of high-quality services and an equality-boosting employer – against a lean managerial state outsourcing public services to the private sector, cutting bureaucratic slack and superfluous workers, and running public entities more like companies. From the start, new public management discourse and strategies were shaped by business scholars and consultancies, but also by the International Monetary Fund or the OECD, introducing their own interests into recommendations for more business-like public authorities. Long before the advent of AITs, these initiatives turned citizens into consumers rather than rights-holders and public services into offers whose legitimacy depends on value-for-money instead of public good considerations (rhetorically, at the very least, but also strictly material in many cases where welfare cuts went hand in hand with a leaner state).

For now, Elon Musk's early 2025 cost-cutting drive in the US federal government has been the pinnacle of this trend, with state employees sacked for "underperformance" and (allegedly) replaced by AI systems. Even though it proved temporary, the alliance between the world's richest and the world's most powerful men has been as troubling as it has been US-specific in its extremeness. More broadly conceived, just how much public sector work is framed through a techno-managerial lens depends on national institutions. In countries with a more positive view of state-provided services and public employment (think Scandinavia) automation in welfare services works less to reduce levels and quality of service provision than it does in liberal welfare states such as the UK.[42] And in cultures that cherish an ethics of care, like South Korea, using AITs to improve support for vulnerable citizens may trump uses for disciplining those depending on state benefits.[43]

AI as a work(er) management tool

When AITs are used to manage and monitor workers, that too has political-economic implications. Such use commodifies labour further, aided by smart performance tracking and task allocation tools. While it has been readily bought and sold in the past, labour as a human activity becomes even more market-driven. From the perspective of workers, it demeans the work, creates alienation and thereby loosens the bonds between workers, the labour they provide, and their loyalty to whomever employs them at any given moment. This can create a vicious circle. As alienation damages a worker's intrinsic motivation, employers may feel compelled to use even more tech to keep tabs on their employees or to build tech-based incentive structures around them that combine carrots and sticks, deepening alienation yet further. As we discuss here, institutions can also mitigate such deleterious dynamics.

Employers use algorithmic worker management for a variety of ends: it features in hiring, directing work, organizing workflows, controlling individual workers, and evaluating and (eventually) sacking workers. AI hiring commonly ranks applications, only forwarding the most promising ones.[44] Going further, companies like Neotas offer online screening of potential and current employees (including job applicants) by sifting through their online footprint. Applicants and employees may have little choice but to submit to these intrusive measures as otherwise, they may be suspected of "having something to hide" and might not be invited for an interview or they might be fired. Whether that is possible depends on the jurisdiction in question, of course: legal worker protection plays a central role in determining whether bosses can use these kinds of tools to screen their workers and discipline or fire them if they do not like what they find.

Automated interviewing tools take this a step further, with companies like HireVue providing AI-driven assessments to analyse a candidate's facial expressions, verbal patterns or word choices in video interviews, often recorded automatically without a human being on the company-side of the screen. While these tools claim to offer more objective evaluations compared to a human interviewer, as for any AIT, their performance hinges on their training data. This may well reinforce existing social biases: penalizing non-native speakers, neurodivergent applicants or those who do not conform to an expected style of speaking. The decision-making of such AITs remains opaque, often leaving interviewees with little chance of recourse if they are unfairly rejected. The risks of discriminatory practices pervading the labour market has led the EU, for example, to categorize recruitment and employment among the "high-risk" AIT use cases which require close monitoring, documentation, certification and a higher degree of explainability. And while the effectiveness of such protections remains an open question, job seekers are probably even worse off where these are not in place at all.

For capital owners, authoritarian states and employers, labour is also a source of unrest that jeopardizes the control of production processes, economic profits, and also the stability of political regimes (another dimension often sidelined by narrow productivity talk). While some suggest that workers might also get hold of new tools to organize and voice collective dissent through digital technologies – a strategy called "*sous*veillance" such as the social media campaigns surfacing around the Google walkouts[45] – power asymmetries are such that workers in most places draw the short straw in comparison to states and employees. The deployment of surveillance tech in authoritarian contexts has been welcomed as a way to reduce regimes' vulnerability to pressure or even insurrection from those usually doing the dirty surveillance and enforcement work on the streets (the secret police or the army).[46] And in countries such as China we already observe a correlation of higher robot density in industrial districts where there is also more labour unrest, suggesting that automation can be a strategy to curb workers' ability to claim higher wages or better working conditions.[47]

Where workers cannot be replaced, tight workplace monitoring can make them more docile. Workplace surveillance itself is not new (think of the panoptic design of the first English textile factories), and it was never only about productivity gains or avoiding hazardous behaviour like smoking near textiles or engines. It was also about social and political control: those who gather in the breaks might be planning a strike, after all. AI enables the simultaneous observation of everyone all the time, for example by analysing screenshots of workers' computers. A lot of so-called productivity software (like the ubiquitous Microsoft Teams) has worker surveillance functionality built into it, for example to analyse emails automatically or otherwise monitor and automatically report on worker activity. Bespoke software suites are even more intrusive.

As the name suggests, productivity tools are at least marketed with the promise of increasing output per worker – something that, to be fair, some tools genuinely achieve. One way to do that, however, is by identifying "slack" in people's working days, trying to "optimize" how they use their working time.[48] Here, workplace surveillance recalibrates an implicit deal between employers and workers which, for example, included a certain amount of downtime at work, in which workers could arrange private things from behind their desk (like ordering something online) or socialize with colleagues. Using AI to shrink downtime effectively squeezes workers more and dissolves the social glue of workplaces, which may itself be an important productivity factor.

What employers (and governments) can do with AI tools varies widely across workplaces and jurisdictions. And so does the extent to which workers can negotiate the terms and conditions of AI deployment at work. For example, EU GDPR rules count as a global privacy gold standard that also protects workers against workplace surveillance. In practice, enforcement is limited and activated only once someone brings a case. As a result, the rules are routinely ignored.[49] Creating a fuss with your boss is risky, certainly when intrusions look comparably innocuous, like vague provisions about workplace monitoring. Power differentials mean that workers can still experience pressure to "consent" to surveillance practices and working conditions that they really would rather avoid.

Performance tracking also comes into play away from offices – think of tech that continuously monitors and "aids" police officers, whether through predictive policing or bodycams. Automated suggestions or outright instructions limit the discretion officers have in their work. Likewise, AI in the public sector is often justified by the promise of avoiding human misjudgements and standardizing how frontline staff (be they police officers, teachers or social benefit case workers) use their discretion. In practice, workers often bypass recommendation systems or protest against their introduction head-on, suggesting that some at least feel unduly micromanaged by AITs. The same is true for algorithmic management in retail, where automated systems tell employees by the minute what to do through the omnipresent earpiece.

There is a hidden downside to AI-powered commodification and intensifying control of labour: it loosens the social ties between employers and workers. If workers are replaceable and by default suspicious (and therefore in need of constant monitoring), so are employers. The alignment between the two suffers. Employers have fewer incentives to train workers when the latter might apply somewhere else the next day: indeed, it spurs precisely the deskilling and standardization of tasks that make workers even more footloose. As workers' emotional attachment and loyalty decreases, they have fewer incentives to invest in a company and to acquire specialized skills or knowledge. Again, these dynamics vary by sector, generating another layer of labour market segmentation: in addition to requiring high levels of specialization and cognitive flexibility, building complex things like satellites or doing interdisciplinary ground research at a public university flourish through trust relationships among employees and employers. In contrast, an AI-driven squeeze that destroys trust and dents worker performance will be less of a concern in a call centre, logistics hub or data annotation firm, where work is already highly compartmentalized and individuals replaceable.

AI also feeds exploitative arm's length working relationships, often summarized under the heading "gig work". That includes setups in which companies buy labour incidentally, typically through digital platforms. Alternatively, platforms bring together many sellers and many buyers. These arrangements have emerged with and depend on digital technologies more generally. The question for us is how AITs specifically fit into this picture. Do they add an extra twist to the business models?

To the degree that AI promotes self-employment for gig workers, it puts them in direct and continuous rivalry, creating incentives to undercut and outpace each other.[50] AI also shapes how ratings and reputations get translated into chances to find work. Even as workers try to outsmart algorithms and customers, for example by strategically manipulating their online profiles and avatars, they still compete with each other.[51] Any task can be awarded only once. When workers try to circumvent this collective action problem through collective bargaining, they may face legal obstacles. Self-employed workers are one-person businesses, and jointly setting prices for their services may run up against antitrust rules. Legal frameworks thus make a central difference. Early in 2024, the EU adopted the Platform Work Directive, which pushes back against the frequent legal fiction of those workers' "independence". The directive forces Uber, for example, to prove that its drivers are not de facto employees, in the sense that the platform controls and directs their work. It also limits which data employers are allowed to collect about workers, including about potential unionization. Limiting the impact of AI-powered labour platforms is a question of political will and power struggle as much as of the tech itself.

Algorithmic control looms large in the data annotation sector that underpins much of the current growth of model accuracy through data cleaning, enrichment and labelling tasks. As research on the history of data work highlights, annotation originated from scientific labs where highly trained researchers performed the job. Its transformation into "a form of dispersed labour that can be outsourced to gig workers" in distant locations required, from the viewpoint of the leading labs harvesting clean data across complex supply chains, "new organizational repertoires of bureaucratic, centralized, and algorithmic control that each made data annotation more dispersible".[52] An example here is ImageNet, a dataset of almost 14.2 million annotated images in 10,000 categories mainly produced through gig work on Amazon Mechanical Turk in 2009: "[to] replace 10 well-trained, collocated graduate students under close supervision with 49,000 unskilled, untrained, geographically dispersed MTurk workers across the US and India, the labour of annotation must be divided into microtasks that can be managed through a single web interface, carried out in parallel to each other, and efficiently evaluated for quality control".[53] In this case, algorithmic evaluations of the quality of data annotation work have a dual effect on labour: they enable replacing more highly trained knowledge workers and supervisors in (usually Western) lab contexts, and they render possible an automated corset of microtask control of the gig work that has thus been relocated across the globe.

Platform workers themselves, at times, have a different view from the critical academics depicting them as hapless victims of exploitative forces. Juliet Schor and her collaborators interviewed Americans working gig jobs, for example delivery drivers for supermarkets (DoorDash or InstaCart) or ride-hailing through Uber or Lyft.[54] They found a broad spectrum of attitudes, from embracing platform work as refreshingly flexible to its rejection and resistance to it. This variation in orientations is often rooted in an overall ideological orientation: the embrace or rejection of a "liberal" entrepreneurial spirit, much like the bigger normative questions we discussed above. Similar findings abound in African, Latin American and Southeast-Asian contexts, where workers appreciated the flexibility and autonomy that comes with just needing any old vehicle, a smartphone, or a PC with internet access (and no formal employer) to generate an income.[55]

Complicating this further, workers in Schor and colleagues' study saw the risky side in this kind of work not so much coming from the platform companies that somehow demeaned their work, but from the customers who would treat them disrespectfully. And indeed, Uber is not directly responsible for arrogant partygoers vomiting in the back of someone's private car and then jumping out without apology. Arguably, however, the commodification of labour that platforms promote may well feed the antisocial behaviour that workers experience. In that sense, the risks workers face are structurally rooted in the stripping away of thicker social relations through platforms.

In any case, the American studies that show workers appreciating what the platforms offer them deserve to be taken with a pinch of salt. Labour rights and bargaining power are notoriously weak in the US, making it unsurprising that platform work can seem an appealing option. Its relative attractiveness also indicates how uninviting (or simply unavailable) the alternatives are. It is no surprise, then, that platform work is clouded in plenty of doublespeak.[56] The nature of the beast is occluded through terms like the sharing economy, the gig economy (with its ring of artistic adventure), partnerships, tasks, independent suppliers, fees (rather than hidden wages), and so on. Pushing back against such language itself is already an important form of resistance.

The power asymmetries between workers and employers are indisputable. How legitimate they are or not is a different question. It hangs on whether we find it appropriate for public authorities to intervene in economic affairs. With the Platform Work Directive just mentioned, the EU claimed the (highly contested) right to intervene in an area that elsewhere is considered off limits for governments. And not only that: in the background hovers the question of (global) solidarity. In a class-based society, those at the top may actually benefit from and happily countenance the precarity of those serving them their ordered food, cleaning their houses, driving them around, and so on. This is not just about a pro- or anti-state intervention attitude in general, but also about class interests: how much appetite is there to intervene in the specific issues on the table? There may be a huge political outcry when professional jobs are on the line, but indifference when lower-class workers suffer, especially if they are located far away in Indonesia or Venezuela (from the perspective of Europe, for example). Individuals' and societies' stances on this issue shape to what degree politics is used to push back against AITs that exacerbate power asymmetries and render the social relation that is labour increasingly asocial and inhumane.

6

Uneven effects in the rest of the world

US and Chinese AI dominance granted, we shift our perspective finally to the global AI landscape, in all its unevenness. Techno-optimists hail the AI roll-out around the world as universally beneficial. But the advanced LLMs from the likes of OpenAI, Meta or DeepSeek could neither have been concocted nor scaled up from any other place. The size of these firms easily overshadows the GDPs of some of the world's poorer countries. Technological leadership is unambiguously out of reach for all but a few countries. The same is true for global AI governance. By 2024, only two low-income countries (Rwanda and Ethiopia) and another 15 lower-middle-income economies (for example, Ghana, Nigeria, Sri Lanka, Uzbekistan and Zambia) had even developed basic AI strategies, compared to 41 high-income and 18 upper-middle-income countries.[1] AI is overwhelmingly a rich country's game.

That said, to what extent do the interactions between US and Chinese powerhouses and "the rest of the world" follow one generalizable pattern? This framing already hints at a common but dangerous cognitive trap: from the perspective of rich countries, everyone else falls under "the rest of the world", as if that were a minor residual category. It is not. Even if we take the whole OECD world and China together, their combined population is less than a third of the global total. "The rest" is where most people live: it is the majority world.

Putting on an economic geography hat, we explore the global ripple effects of highly concentrated AI development across three political economy axes: geoeconomic competition and catch-up races involving a few richer economies, norms-based alliance-building efforts in global tech diplomacy, and the reproduction of colonial and imperial dynamics, including through local actors' complacency or buy-in. It turns out that the universal dynamics of *the* AI transformation, in the singular, are refracted through the prisms of tech-related imaginaries, institutional settings and legacies, and local forms of agency. This dance between universal dynamics and their space-specific articulations creates variegated AI experiences across the globe.

Competing: the geoeconomics of the AI race (among a few)

US and Chinese AI dominance has triggered sundry reactions elsewhere, from funding to governance strategies, as states have responded to geoeconomic dynamics. We unfold them in several steps. To begin with, we dissect how first-mover advantages in tech development have spurred an AI race between the US and China. Afraid of losing out, countries with sufficiently deep pockets and existing tech clusters (including in the EU, India, Israel, the UK and the UAE) are adamant about catching up – irrespective of how realistic that may be.

Joseph Schumpeter first expounded first-mover advantages in his *Theory of Economic Development*: those innovating on existing markets or creating entirely new segments enjoy an advantage over latecomers not only by cashing in early profits but also by controlling the intellectual property and know-how to cement their pole positions. As discussed in Chapter 4, when AI is integrated in existing markets, first movers and those with access to proprietary data can benefit most. But first-mover advantages operate not only within and across economic sectors but also across borders. In generative AI development, business analysts typically assume that early adoption gives national economies a competitive advantage and widens the gap between them and the rest.

This dynamic unfolds around a key feature of the AI stack: AITs are layered onto other digital markets, in many of which US and Chinese companies already lead. Those holding the keys to data, intellectual property, computing power, skills and expertise can jumpstart AI value generation and frustrate others' ambitions. When the Canadian-built AlexNet algorithm won an image recognition competition to much publicity in 2012 – sparking an initial wave of machine learning hype – it was not the decades-old algorithm itself that drew attention, but its pairing with unprecedented amounts of data and computing power.[2] Big AI could build on pre-existing market concentration in digital tech.

When countries build first-mover advantages on top of massive market power, it hollows out their claims about "universally beneficial AI". As Global South observers highlight, anyone hoping to enter these markets would compete with "multi-billion dollar corporations, which already dominate the market, enjoy the benefit of network effects, have accumulated brand equity and trade secrets, and have the power to acquire smaller companies".[3] And, we should add, exclusive access to vast data and computing power.

The combination of economic and geopolitical race dynamics has unleashed large-scale investment globally. At the most martial end, Vladimir Putin promoted AI leadership as the key to global domination in front of students in Yaroslavl in 2017. But he is not alone in his ambitions. By 2020, around 50 countries had positioned themselves vis-à-vis the Sino-American struggle over AI tech leadership, publishing their own strategies and pumping money into domestic tech infrastructures and startup scenes.[4] Fifty wannabe AI leaders may sound like a large club, but the fact that most countries of the world do not even have a national AI strategy highlights the exclusivity of that club. Many countries lack a coherent AI policy to begin with – a fact often ignored in global competitiveness rhetoric. As a matter of fact, no African country published an AI strategy between 2017 and 2020.

While most countries do not feature in this geopolitical race in the first place, investment potential and institutional variation shape the relative position of those who do. According to an index that maps countries' leadership potential across data, (public) rules, capital and innovation, the UK, Japan, a few EU countries, Canada, Australia and South Korea are top-ranked behind the two global leaders (with a significant gap between the US and China).[5] The most highly ranked country from the Global South is India, followed by Brazil, Argentina and Malaysia. The disaggregation of indicators in this index singles out the "capital" dimension (understood as the "human, financial, diversity and digital foundations" for AI production) as the main factor behind richer OECD countries' leading positions. The enormous investment in infrastructure and skills that sets the US and Chinese economies apart is also a gamechanger for those wanting to catch up.

For Europe, the EU Commission laments "low and fragmented" investment compared to the US and China and bemoans brain drain towards Silicon Valley as stumbling blocks for a more "competitive environment".[6] As "European industry cannot miss the train", the Commission recast its role (and the aim of its regulation and funding decisions) as promoting AI take-up across the continent.[7] Commission President Ursula von der Leyen promised a CERN equivalent for AI (a world-class research site heavily funded by the EU, bringing together top scientists and developers) early during the 2024–29 legislature. In February 2025, the Commission followed up with plans to "mobilise €200 billion for investment in AI, including a new European fund of €20 billion for AI gigafactories".[8] Whether the EU can muster the political will and resources to follow through with these plans is a completely different matter, of course.

Across the Channel, a close observer of British AI policy finds that London's rhetoric and strategy papers on AI reproduce "a fantasy of independence that masks deeper structural dependence on […] funding and infrastructures provided by Silicon Valley", fuelled by pride about "brushing shoulders with the US and China" in global AI leadership rankings.[9] London's National AI Strategy sets a ten-year plan "to make Britain a global AI superpower", hoping to expand genuinely homegrown AI (with the US-owned lab DeepMind driving most of the UK startup scene's tech innovation), boost investment, decrease dependency on US-controlled infrastructure, and regain some global regulatory sway that has been lost post-Brexit.[10] An action plan for developing a domestic AI industry – for example, through "unlocking public sector data", the establishment of "AI Growth Zones" (where cheap land and energy can crowd in private investors), or the creation of "UK Sovereign AI" (a unit to coordinate public-private partnerships on tech innovation and "maximise the UK's upside") – is as filled with geopolitical jargon as it is void of commitments to public investments.[11]

India, too, harbours ambitions to forge a local AI ecosystem with an independent computing and startup scene. While full AI "self-reliance" is unlikely given entanglement with US firms, India may have a competitive advantage elsewhere. Large aggregate data pools and their quick growth and accessibility can improve the relative position of leapfrogs in the AI race. India, like Indonesia, trumps European countries on population size and the lack of effective opposition to – or data protection laws against – large government data gathering. As observers of the subcontinent note, "India is attempting to jumpstart AI development by building data platforms mediated and promoted by the state".[12] Projects like the Aadhaar biometric identification system target the entire population, creating business cases for other homegrown and home market targeted AI applications, from public surveillance to the distribution of welfare payments or the administration of elections. In effect, we see an uneasy pact between data gathering for government purposes at the expense of increasing dependence on digital companies, most of which remain foreign.

Fossil-fuelled rentier economies with deep pockets and a need to find the next source of income make for another different type of AI race contestant. The UAE stands out. Some rankings already list it in fourth position in 2024. It can enrol private and state-owned companies' wealth for prestige projects such as Jais, the largest Arabic LLM, catering to potentially 400 million speakers worldwide. Beyond leadership in corners of the generative AI market, however, the UAE's industrial policy mirrors "fantasies of 'absolute sovereignty'" through tech over dissidents or unruly workers at home and as a national security tool in international conflicts.[13] Like other autocratic regimes, the UAE has the dubious freedom to ignore voters' wariness of budgetary priorities or policy coherence. Whether handing out "Golden Visas" to investors and developers from China (the UAE), investing in the US Stargate consortium as the single largest donor (an Abu Dhabi state-owned fund), or building a $5 billion data centre in an artificial desert city (Saudi Arabia), the ability to move fast and spend big unfettered by norms-based alliances or electoral concerns sets Middle Eastern tech leaders apart from their competitors elsewhere.

A noteworthy dynamic in the "race to AI" concerns countries' ability to attract tech expertise against the pull of Silicon Valley or Shenzhen. For example, India tries to retain and regain Indian tech workers: "Although 20 percent of the global chip design workforce is located in India, it almost exclusively works for international companies like Intel, AMD, and Nvidia".[14] That could count as an opportunity of the kind that China has successfully seized in the past. Countries such as Israel and India (and again China before them) benefitted from workers trained in Silicon Valley coming back and building tech clusters at home.[15] For workers, too, this is not solely an economic question. They frequently look for working conditions, welfare provisions and a political culture more attractive than those in the Sino-American clusters, not least as the American political climate has become less welcoming. Luring qualified workers back home is a key prerequisite for successful challenger strategies; that may prove difficult, especially for repressive regimes or war-struck parts of the world.

For now, countries other than the US or China can at best carve out a niche in one of the tech leaders' orbits and integrate AITs into their own economies. Dependencies remain. The few that could become second-tier AI powers with at least a modicum of tech independence will need a viable mix of domestic market size, capital, homegrown expertise, and political will to push ahead. They include India, Japan, South Korea, the UAE, Saudi Arabia and maybe Israel. Brazil has admirable ambitions, but it may well need to partner up with other Latin American countries to have a chance of success. Most others are poised to remain digital dependencies of China or the US, including the UK, which for now seems content with a privileged niche in an American-dominated tech sphere.

EU countries make a special case, given their combined wealth, expertise, infrastructure and market size. As we outlined above, the European Commission and leading member states claim to be serious about building technological independence, including in AI; with sufficient political will and unity, that may just be achievable. Even there, however, dreams of digital sovereignty may run up against trade and especially military dependencies on the US. That the EU would mirror China and the US in their international digital reach, in contrast, seems implausible even in the most optimistic scenarios.

Persuading: ideologies and interests in struggles over AI governance

Any country wanting to develop and govern AITs is, to varying degrees, dependent on what other countries do in this realm.[16] Governments therefore not only influence what happens inside their borders but try to shape AI rules beyond them. The result has been a complex and shifting web of international AI governance initiatives, sometimes involving only two jurisdictions; at other times spanning the globe. Shaping global AI governance is now a crucial plank of countries' competitiveness strategies, at least for those with potential for meaningful influence. Over the course of the 2020s, China, the EU, the US, but also the UK and the UAE, have tried to shape standards for AI production, procurement, commercialization, and use worldwide, aligning them with domestic regulatory preferences to support their own AI sectors.

At the same time, the major global actors try to use fledgling AI governance to portray themselves as being on the right side of unfolding AI history. When China has challenged US tech dominance, liberal democratic leaders have decried Chinese AI development and governance suggesting it threatens democracy and peace, even as the US happily cuts deals with autocratic regimes such as Saudi Arabia. An analysis of AI-related policy documents in China, the EU and the US (under the Biden administration) highlights that the US is, at least on paper, "heavily concerned with protecting their democratic values", with the EU placing more weight on "ethical principles and societal values".[17]

How does international AI governance fit into a political economy view of the field? International AI governance forums are intended not only as laboratories for governance ideas and best practices, but also to disseminate homegrown governance approaches, not least to the benefit of local companies already following these standards. According to the OECD AI Policy Observatory, the US, China and European countries have developed almost half of all national AI regulations, which often serve as blueprints for international negotiations.[18] In comparison, most African nations and – to a lesser extent – Latin American countries are reduced to copycat behaviour and hold little sway in developing global governance. AI rules inevitably diffuse from the leaders in the field to everyone else, leaving governments in the Global South with little agency.

The transatlantic partners (EU and the US) and China took pains to limit the impact of opposing voices on their home turf. This dynamic translated into a battle for dominance in third-country markets.[19] In the early 2020s, Brussels and Washington announced joint AI risk assessment methodologies developed by the then EU-US Trade and Technology Council, a bilateral forum to coordinate tech governance, and hoped for future cooperation with "like-minded countries". On the other side, Xi Jinping welcomed "fellow G20 members" to his world AI conference in 2025, after Beijing had pivoted its Belt and Road Initiative to frontier technologies under the Digital Silk Road label.[20] Jointly, the BRICS – an intergovernmental organization comprising Brazil, Russia, India, China, and South Africa initially, and also including Egypt, Ethiopia, Indonesia, Iran and the UAE – created their own AI study group in a clear move against global AI governance initiatives dominated by Western countries.

At the time, scholars diagnosed "broad alignment" of AI legislative initiatives in the US and EU, with "divisions and preferences of industries and advocacy groups" mostly occurring within each jurisdiction rather than constituting a large transatlantic divide.[21] Until 2024, a shared interest in countering Chinese influence unified the US and Europe. A peek under the hood of transatlantic cooperation, however, already revealed the differing cooperation incentives of the US and the EU. Under Trump 1.0, the US had little interest in coordinating AI policy with the Europeans. The Biden administration rekindled transatlantic cooperation, effectively hoping to enlist Europe in a Washington-led anti-China digital tech alliance. References to shared values such as democracy and human rights bolstered the effort. From the European side, things looked a little different. Compared to what happened in the US, governance was clearly more norm-driven, reflected in talk about human-centric AI in line with European fundamental rights. As our own research on EU regulatory rhetoric shows, Brussels' pitch for stronger in-house development and regulation of "trustworthy AI" had also been justified with the promotion of an alternative business and governance model to the Chinese, and to a lesser extent the American, approach. "Undemocratic uses" of AI tech, such as social scoring systems and forms of mass surveillance, were to be banned in the European common market as a moral message to the world that "this is not our vision of Europe" and that "we are not China".[22]

A "norm-based alliance" was thus music to the ears of many Brussels policymakers and transatlantic cooperation could have proven a key vehicle to diffuse EU rules, which were developed at that time and eventually crystallized in the AI Act. Global influence-seeking had extended beyond attempts to sell "homemade" AI applications or to standardize AITs in ways benefitting national economic interests. It has also been conditioned by a clash of governance approaches, rhetorically justified by competing ideologies and narratives. Externally, the European narratives of more democratic AI futures legitimized alliance-building and protectionist moves against adversaries; internally, they signalled to citizens that societal values indeed loom large in AI development and that spending public money on AI was indeed urgent and legitimate. This dynamic fell apart with Trump 2.0, a point to which we return below.

While ideological differences can partly explain alternative regulatory foci and alliances in AI governance, they have also been embedded (and often become discursive weaponry) in a global tech economy shaped by logics of capitalist extraction, economic competition and geopolitical struggle. The previous chapters have repeatedly highlighted these factors in US tech policy, making it useful to take a closer look at China, too. Since Xi gained power in 2012, China has increased its influence in international relations by portraying itself as "the champion of the developing world", promoting socio-economic development across the globe as a nominally anti-colonial struggle.[23] In his address to the 2024 G20 summit, President Xi claimed that "international governance and cooperation on artificial intelligence (AI) should be strengthened, to make sure that AI is for good and for all".[24] The implicit enemy here is a global tech market dominated by US Big Tech. In a more direct attack, the Chinese government's AI Governance Strategy has played the strings of global equality, castigating US dominance and offering itself as an alternative partner for tech development cooperation:

> All countries, regardless of their size, strength, or social system, should have equal rights to develop and use AI. […] [International AI governance should be] based on exchange and cooperation and with full respect for differences in policies and practices among countries. […] We should increase the representation and voice of developing countries in global AI governance, and ensure equal rights, equal opportunities, and equal rules for all countries in AI development and governance. Efforts should be made to conduct international cooperation with and provide assistance to developing countries, to bridge the gap in AI and its governance capacity.[25]

In this context, the Belt and Road Science, Technology and Innovation Cooperation Action Plan aims to "increase of the number of joint laboratories built with other parties to 100" by 2028, and to support "young scientists from other countries to work on short-term programs in China".[26] President Xi has been unusually open about China's strategic self-interest in what might seem like an altruistic AI development agenda. In (literally) flowery rhetoric, he found that "when you give roses to others, their fragrance lingers on your hand. In other words, helping others is also helping oneself".[27]

This rhetorical focus on China helping the oppressed also resurfaces in Chinese companies' expansion strategies. An analysis of Transsion's patent applications for facial recognition technologies highlights the innovative potential of "enrolling more dark-skinned faces into the datasets" and correcting "the distorted machine vision for dark skin" as a matter of "inclusive representation".[28] Such rhetoric can fall on fertile ground beyond the confines of political regime blocs. Many countries in the majority world (democratically governed or not) see China as a role model for socio-economic development, sparking a pragmatic desire to repeat its successes.

Chinese tech diplomacy may be coated with lofty global equality rhetoric, but it harbours a geoeconomic competitiveness logic at its core. Investment in frontier tech in third countries is attractive for Beijing because it "present[s] less risk, lower operating costs, and faster returns than traditional infrastructure projects".[29] Such returns include, for example, no- or low-cost testing grounds for Chinese AI companies. CloudWalk Technology, for example, could hone its facial recognition system's ability to recognize darker skin tones through a Digital Silk Road trial project "at key entry/exit points and transport hubs in Zimbabwe".[30]

American government consultants and regulators have typically portrayed AI governance options as a binary choice between good and bad. US-based security analysts, for example, warn that China pursues a "proliferation-first approach to international AI norm-setting, focusing on aggressively building Chinese AI tech into developing economies ahead of pushing specific regulations internationally".[31] Such strategies obviously clash with American attempts to solidify or extend its own digital dominance. Tech-related geopolitical struggles, like the earlier Cold War space race, have found a new enemy in China, and the emerging Sino-American rivalry shapes global governance forums (for example, in the standard-setting organization, the International Telecommunication Union) as much as it does national funding decisions and policies.

To counter this perceived threat, the US has not only invested heavily in homegrown infrastructure but also "weaponized the institutional divergences of China's variety of digital capitalism to impose sanctions on Chinese transnational high-tech companies".[32] Through directly targeting Chinese Big Tech with its regulations, including export controls for advanced chips, and pressuring diplomatic allies to embargo Chinese tech, the US has sought to decouple itself and its allies from Beijing.

In the transatlantic alliance, the EU–US Trade and Technology Council has been the most tangible effort, focused on a whole gamut of digital policies including data transfers and the extraterritorial implications of the EU's Digital Markets and Digital Services Acts. Its early statements on AI unambiguously criticized autocratic uses of AI, pointing to worries about a Chinese social credit system as an example. (General worries about AI abuse for population surveillance are appropriate enough. But both in transatlantic and in EU-internal debates, the social credit system has frequently been an argumentative trope for setting one's own actions apart as morally superior, regardless of on the ground realities in China, Europe and North America.)[33]

The Trade and Technology Council never lived up to its promise, even before Donald Trump resumed office. In AI matters, federal legislative action in the US remained unlikely as long as President Biden confronted a Republican-dominated Congress. In the meantime, the EU detailed its regulatory approach in the AI Act, effectively tying itself to a fixed set of rules. With many details unspecified in the AI Act, there remained theoretical room for regulatory alignment. But priorities on both sides of the Atlantic shifted away from bilateral cooperation: in Washington, Chinese advances in AI were seen with increasing alarm, denting any willingness to be held back in trans-Pacific competition by prevaricating Europeans. In Brussels, internal coordination absorbed increasing attention, with AI Act details needing to be filled in and enforcement a challenge.

Once Trump returned to the White House and announced his America-first approach to tech policy, little was left of proactive regulatory alignment and cooperation. European Commission President von der Leyen did not even mention the US as a like-minded partner at the February 2025 AI Action Summit, setting the notion of "cooperative AI" as one where everyone benefits: "Cooperative AI can be attractive well beyond Europe, including for our partners in the Global South. [...] AI can be a gift to humanity. But we must make sure that benefits are widespread and accessible to all".[34] A narrowly self-interested unilateralism had returned and close regulatory cooperation – especially of the kind that would entail concessions by the US – vanished from the agenda.

The weakening transatlantic alliance has been reflected in a waning emphasis on "democratic norms" in US AI governance efforts. President Biden energetically supported US tech giants' investment in the autocratically-run Gulf States, for example when Microsoft injected $15 billion in G42, an Abu Dhabi AI group.[35] More recently, Donald Trump has embraced UAE and Saudi Arabia as AI allies in America's mission to outcompete China despite ideological differences with the Gulf States. Meanwhile, the Gulf States hope to become independent tech players, not least driven by the need to replace fossil fuel revenues and renew the promise of social security and prosperity that has legitimized autocratic rule.

Trying to "play both sides" in the Sino-American rivalry, the leverage of countries such as the UAE in global AI governance may well increase. For example, whereas some BRICS states – most notably Russia, who created a Technology Investment Fund with China in 2021 – are clearly aligned with China in global AI governance, other powers such as Brazil, India, South Africa and the more recent addition UAE, are wary about taking sides, seeing it as a risk to their own tech development. In Latin America, where history has entrenched both linkages with and also dependence on the US, many leaders remain wary of Big Tech entreaties, too. In the meantime, India seeks invest-ment from both American and Chinese firms to bolster its national ecosystem and has toned down its appetite for strict AI regulation, even while entertain-ing its own Trade and Technology Council with the EU. Meanwhile, a Brazilian senator with NASA ties lobbied against a stricter domestic AI bill directly in Silicon Valley, fearing that such regulation would kill the country's nascent tech industry.[36] Again, tensions between any country's tech catch-up strategy and its cooperation within the BRICS context could mean that only the strong-est players in the bloc financially and politically (currently India, the UAE, and Saudi Arabia) can make an impact.

Considering this, what are we to make of those international governance initiatives that have at least generated clear outputs, such as the Council of Europe Framework Convention on AI or the Hiroshima Principles on AI, adopted by the G7? A sober assessment seems in order. Agreed principles and declarations do not commit governments to anything. Vague principles dom-inate, often without any determination to follow through. AI governance opti-mists had assumed that agreement on high-level principles would be a prelude to more detailed and binding commitments. With the benefit of hindsight, much of what has been "agreed" looks like immaterial posturing. Even the sole "hard" agreement on AI – the Council of Europe's Framework Convention on AI – invites scepticism: by the time it was signed, the EU had already adopted its AI Act, meaning that nothing in the Convention would commit EU mem-ber states to actions inimical to its rules. To garner American support for the Convention, the EU also agreed that its reach would be limited to what gov-ernments do with AI, letting private companies off the hook. Even then, it was clear from the beginning that a Republican-dominated Congress would never ratify this Convention, and with Trump's return to the White House even a vague normative symbolism of a US signature is gone.

The one form of international cooperation that is more consequential is standard setting. In the AI-specific working groups of the International Organization for Standardization and the International Electrotechnical Commission, which work jointly in this domain, technical standards are set that matter directly to companies and thereby also to their home governments. AI standards may end up codifying politically contentious concepts such as "freedom from bias" or safety testing procedures, and by aligning with some companies' business models more than with others, standards themselves tilt the economic playing field. Standard setting, in short, is itself a domain of AI politics. Widely accepted standards do shape whole industries, and when trade is otherwise open, they can erect significant non-tariff barriers. At the same time, standards such as those developed by the two organizations mentioned previously are voluntary unless mandated for use by domestic legislation.

Their impact will thus depend on how fragmented the global AI market will turn out to be: it is currently too early to tell.

Taken together, governance cooperation and alliance formation are neither neat nor binary; instead, they follow the politics of the day and instrumentalize existing institutions, ideologies and narratives. For the time being, the international interactions around AI have returned to a more hard-nosed logic of empire building rather than a genuine sense of international cooperation, even the kind guided by enlightened self-interest.

Colonial and imperial dynamics: AI leaders and the majority world

Discussions about global AI transformations usually have a narrow focus with the rich and technologically advanced countries leading the charge. If mentioned at all, countries outside that small circle typically find themselves at the receiving end of tech development and global regulatory efforts, often reduced to imitation with neither sufficient appetite nor capacity to steer AI futures.[37] The fact that these countries are seriously behind in this regard does not simply indicate a lack technological innovation or will to become AI leaders. Instead, patterns of economic domination resonate with earlier, exploitative periods of global economic history, leading some analysts to identify a new phase of digital colonialism in our times.[38] Seen through a decolonial lens, the spatial concentration of tech development and related economic gains, the geopolitical competition around AITs and their regulation and the increasing securitization of these technologies both feed on and accentuate uneven socio-spatial relationships in global capitalism.

But is history simply repeating itself with African or Latin American communities "cast [...] in the eternal role of the miner", rather than adding value to available domestic raw materials, data and labour?[39] Our answer is both yes and no. Talk of "AI imperialism" or "data colonialism" in the singular misleadingly suggests that "the" majority world is exposed to the whims of Sino-American tech diffusion in a universal and passive manner. Instead, AI transformations take very different forms as they interact with contingent legacies and political economy constellations.

To sharpen the analysis, we distinguish three dynamics that operate simultaneously but should not be conflated: first, colonial legacies continue to affect which countries have the economic resources, highly educated workers and political leverage to become at least regional AI leaders. Not every former colonial power is an AI frontrunner, but in Africa especially, colonial legacies continue to hamper well-funded, homegrown tech development. Second, in colonial dynamics AI leaders use other typically poorer regions of the world as sites to extract raw materials, exceedingly cheap labour and data. These colonial dynamics today are frequently practiced by countries other than the traditional colonial powers (so by the US and China rather than the UK, France, Spain or Portugal). The central feature is an AI policy that treats other countries as repositories of input for domestic AI development, without much concern for the wellbeing of people or the target countries' economies. Imperial strategies, finally, are not about getting things out of other countries, but getting one's companies in by occupying markets through the creation of digital dependencies.

These three facets of asymmetrical relations can go together, but they do not have to. As has been true for past colonial and imperial projects, the relationships between companies and governments – both in the economic centres and in subordinated locales – is complex and highly varied. Some local actors are coopted into domineering relationships; others resist. That makes it important to write local forms of agency in the majority world (including political complacency) back into an overly simplistic story of Sino-American domination.

To consider colonial legacies first, riches accumulated through colonialism (and settler-colonialism in North America) have propelled economies in some parts of the world to lead digital markets, while depleting colonized territories of skills, craftsmanship and natural resources. Lack of electricity and internet access, along with a massively underfunded university sector in Africa, are both the legacy of colonial extraction and impediments for AI innovation today.[40] For some self-declared AI "leapfrogs" (an admittedly optimistic self-description), catching up is not only about economic prosperity and national sovereignty. It is also an attempt to correct entrenched asymmetries and injustices in the global political economy, many of which have roots in past European colonialism. The Brazilian government frames homegrown AI and involvement in global standardization as a way to "bring the country past a level of dependency and backwardness to one of leadership".[41] In a similar vein, in South Africa constitutional commitment "to rectifying historical injustices" from its colonial and apartheid legacy informs an industrial policy approach to tech development.[42]

American and Chinese Big Tech projects in the majority world echo both the old narrative of colonizers as enlightened civilizers and saviours and the exploitative land- and labour-grabbing of traditional colonialism. From the sixteenth century onwards, myths of "discoveries" and "uncharted" land, the dispossession of local communities and their labour, and narratives of European superiority had shaped capitalist expansion. Abeba Birhane sees such accounts mirrored in the "colonial rhetoric" of "connecting the unconnected" and "creating knowledge about Africa's population distribution" in Facebook's population density map of Africa – a project facilitated with an algorithmic integration of computer vision, satellite images, population and social media data.[43] Digital empire building today is justified, even hailed, through the benefits it supposedly brings the locals, even as market expansion remains the sole concern for most tech companies.

In such colonial dynamics, data, labour and raw materials are extracted from the Global South for a pittance by multinationals while sophisticated AI-powered products and services (for example, LLMs or FRTs) are sold back to these countries. Along the way, the digital technologies dominated by foreign companies seep ever more deeply into the economic, societal and political tissue of peripheral countries. AI applications in agriculture – such as predictive tools for what to plant and when to harvest – can make local firms more productive but also entrench the dominance of agri-behemoths such as John Deere, threatening local economies of smallholder farming. Equally, AITs to make microcredits or childcare benefits in Kenya or Nigeria more cost-effective and targeted may or may not benefit vulnerable populations. But in the meantime, they do load the pockets of tech suppliers.

The exploitative extraction of raw materials and labour has gained an additional dimension in our data-hungry digital age. "Data territories" are a new (virtual and yet spatially situated) feature of how colonial dynamics unfold.[44] To be sure, data extraction happens worldwide. The US government kick-started the first comprehensive image databases with pictures of residents; mugshots of criminal suspects and prison inmates have widely been used in early algorithm training, too. By treating data as "abundant" for anyone to grab for governance or business purposes, regulators made the profitable rise of FRTs possible in the first place. "Data colonialism" covers not just citizens in the majority world, but everyone who leaves traces such as fingerprints, retina scans, video-taped faces, bank transactions, or social media posts on a data territory just waiting to be commercially exploited without any financial compensation.

Still, the universal data-extractivist logic cannot obscure the spatial disparities in where it hits hardest. Birhane suggests that profit maximizing tech corporations have a particular interest in extracting data from seemingly "unconnected" (or rather, behaviourally unmapped) territories and populations.[45] These territories frequently lack data protection and privacy laws, which might safeguard citizens in Europe, for example, from more intrusive practices. In Africa, excessive data extraction often hides behind a façade of bringing tech innovation to pressing problems.

Gig workers' exploitation for data labelling and model training also feeds on global labour market inequalities. Workers in Latin America, Southeast Asia and Africa in particular rely on precarious AI-producing jobs and gigs. Such work happens within AI power centres as well. Chinese vocational students, for example, are vulnerable to be pressured into exploitative AI assembly line "internships" in data annotation centres.[46] In the European case, microwork is concentrated in countries with relatively high unemployment rates such as Italy, Spain and Portugal.[47]

Governments in the majority world are often ready to compromise on labour protections in an effort to tackle large-scale unemployment. Homegrown companies' ambitions to secure a share of the global AI industry also work against tight rules. In Africa, where populations are much younger than in Europe, China, Japan or the US, the pressure is particularly intense. In Kenya, for instance, one million new job seekers enter an already tight labour market each year. Many governments are then happy to promise job creation in booming "AI sweatshops", as one Kenyan civil rights activist called them in a *60 Minutes* documentary, and reluctant to enforce stricter labour laws.[48] Kenya-based data annotation intermediary Sama reportedly hires workers on precarious short-term contracts (sometimes just for a day), imposes extreme deadlines, withholds pay and denies mental health support to data labellers exposed to traumatizing content such as suicide or child abuse. In the meantime, there is no meaningful oversight from the Nairobi government or major clients such as OpenAI.[49]

AI-first firms benefit from African, Latin American or South-Asian AI sweatshops to make their model breakthroughs possible. But when economic and job aspirations – like those driving "Silicon Savannah", Nairobi's tech hub – trump workers' and citizens' rights, local governments also bear responsibility. Job creation and foreign investment strategies that neglect labour protections and local corporate accountability risk making governments complicit in exploitation across the AI stack. History has left many economies in the majority world dependent on foreign capital and employment. Breaking this vicious cycle may thus require robust enforcement of AI companies' corporate responsibility throughout the value chain, similar to previous efforts to address labour abuses in the global garment industry.

When we focus on colonial dynamics and imperial strategies, we see clear parallels between US and Chinese Big Tech fanning out across the globe and the global asymmetries and inequalities reinforced in their wake. Once more consider Chinese smartphone developer Transsion, which has built the largest database of dark-skinned facial images worldwide and uses it in smartphone apps optimized to recognize dark skin. Obviously enough, Transsion is not driven by altruism. Its product development through facial data "sustains its competitive position and how its constellation of hardware and apps are integral to its success in routine experimentation of artificial intelligence, facial recognition, and other emerging areas of computation".[50] And the "unbalanced power relations" between China and most countries at the receiving end of its technologies (particularly in Africa) make it unlikely that a Nigerian or Ghanaian startup would have enough resources to compete with a company like Transsion.[51]

Accounts of US Big Tech's global reach read very similarly, irrespective of White House rhetoric against Beijing. As two seminal works on surveillance capitalism and data colonialism highlight (both with a strong empirical foundation in the practices of Silicon Valley behemoths), data extraction and mass surveillance of internet users are also central in American tech companies' business models.[52] They fuel US-made AI innovations from image and speech recognition to LLMs. Exploring the case of South Africa, Michael Kwet casts US firms as digital imperialists "planting infrastructure in the Global South engineered for their own needs, enabling economic and cultural domination while imposing privatized forms of governance [...] to ensure their own dominance over critical functions in the tech ecosystem".[53]

That said, accounts of digital colonialism or imperialism risk eliding the agency of local communities and actors, whether through joining forces with foreign companies or resistance against them, a point to which we return in Chapter 7. Any shorthand account of how, for example, the myriad Digital Silk Road projects affect any specific African nation would wrongly essentialize these interactions as homogeneous expressions of Chinese tech colonialism. It matters whether a host country government proactively collaborates with Chinese firms to pursue its own authoritarian goals, whether a firm like Microsoft co-opts local leaders with promises of investment and employment, or whether resistance against global AI empires arises from national institutions or social movements. Local communities themselves can be "active mediators" of data extraction and tech development as they "carve out spaces for value creation that are meaningful in their local and national contexts".[54]

Indeed, the extraterritorial dominance of US or Chinese tech companies is often co-produced by firms and politicians in the targeted regions in more space-specific political and economic dynamics. An analysis of Transsion's role in Africa, for example, highlights that "the most successful Chinese projects [of tech diffusion in the Global South] are those in which Africans have active collaborative buy-in".[55] Many examples of Chinese FRTs involve local leaders' authoritarian goals: telecommunication provider ZTE, for example, "provides the Ethiopian government with infrastructure to enable it to monitor communications by opposition activists and journalists".[56] Huawei tech has assisted Ugandan and Zambian leaders to monitor political opponents and Ethiopia is reported to use "mixed surveillance technologies supplied not only by Chinese companies but also by companies from [the] UK, German[y], Italy, and Israel".[57] In this case, it is essential to consider not just the expansionist strategies of tech companies and their home jurisdictions, but also the

Ethiopian government's rationale for buying and deploying this tech, and its rationales for picking providers from multiple digital empires. Plausibly, for some countries "doing business with China does simply not carry the same historical weight as doing business with the old European empires".[58] This can make extractivist tech from Beijing more palatable.

Sometimes, AI development builds on much older population control techniques originating in colonial times. Take India's Aadhaar system, the world's most ambitious biometric identification tool. It combines a statistical method for measuring facial similarity among people of the same region and caste (Mahalanobis's distance function classifies ethnicities based on how similar their facial features are) with US-developed machine learning capacities. This complicates narrow assumptions of Western epistemological dominance in model building. Measurements draw on older socio-ethnic hierarchies in India promoted by local elites during British colonial rule. Such dispersed agency without a single "culprit" matters when the Indian government relies on racial assumptions from colonial times baked into Aadhaar for its contemporary welfare governance and population control. And Mahalanobis's measures for facial features have travelled beyond India and become the fundament for FRTs worldwide. As racialized "statistical reasoning […] and its material antecedents [in colonized India] are looped into contemporary machine-learning", the Aadhaar project blurs any neat boundaries between AI colonizers and the colonized.[59]

A variegated analysis of claims about universal AI transformations also casts doubt on Western tech-pessimistic assumptions, including those of one-way colonialization dynamics. Such accounts obscure the rationales for majority world communities to engage with AITs, even as they remain dominated by a handful of global power hubs. As digital anthropologist Payal Arora finds, youngsters in Bangladesh or Nigeria often view AI and other digital tech positively, as locally designed datasets and apps have already improved their lives by offering educational opportunities and jobs, as well as new ways to socialize and date.[60] Local governments, whose legitimacy often depends on tech's potential to solve societal problems, may be ready to sacrifice (arguably unrealistic) digital sovereignty ambitions to a giant American or Chinese helping hand.

Some majority world countries struggle with basic access to electricity and a stable internet. Even if you have a mobile phone with good connectivity, being able to charge it only once a week will make you think twice before wasting battery life on chats with an LLM. Some pockets of high-tech communities aside, "barriers to AI development and adoption outside the West and the richer countries of the East point to a limited absorptive capacity for AI, in Africa in particular".[61] Consider the almost endearing case of NoMindBhutan.

This startup, run by half a dozen grad students at Gyalpozhing College of Information Technology, provides customized LLM-based solutions to local clients. With the only data centre in the country a mere 2,000 square feet big (compare that to China's biggest, which is 5,000 times as large) and English-speaking LLMs dominating AI service development, the startup remains heavily dependent on tech firms beyond Bhutanese borders.

Such constraints on majority world AI innovation are widespread. To be sure, there are laudable networking efforts meant for the African AI research and startup community to move from "receivers" to "active owners and shapers of these technological advances".[62] South African DataProphet successfully sells its manufacturing-optimizing software internationally, and overall funding for tech startups grew constantly between 2015 and 2022.[63] That said, funding for the African tech entrepreneur scene as a whole remains meagre compared to the deals that startups like OpenAI or Anthropic strike on their own. Startups across the continent acquired over $3.3 billion in their best year (2022, down again to just over $1 billion in 2024). With a population roughly similar to Africa's in size, India's startup funding was five to six times as large.[64] The highest valued African startup Flutterwave (a payment platform not even squarely in the AI business) had an estimated valuation of $3 billion in 2022.[65] To put that in perspective, in 2024 Alphabet, Amazon, Apple, Meta and Microsoft alone were predicted to invest approximately $400 billion in AI-related hardware and research and development.[66] Their combined valuation reached many trillion dollars.

Global South economies with AI ambitions (most importantly India, South Africa and Brazil) thus walk a tightrope between foreign investment, which creates more short-term dependency, and boosting their local AI ecosystem for greater long-term autonomy. When Microsoft invests $3 billion in India, for example, risks of deepening reliance on US-controlled infrastructure appear secondary to New Delhi's desire to morph itself into an AI innovation hub.[67] Similarly, Big Tech companies have prominently funded the African tech hub scene, at least since the mid-2010s. They provide seed financing, labs and mentoring through traineeships and bootcamps for next generation developer-entrepreneurs in Lagos or Nairobi, for instance. This investment includes community-based open source projects such as the development of natural language processing tools for Ghanaian languages with the participation of Google and Microsoft.[68] In the end, the geoeconomic dynamics and competitiveness imperatives that fuel leading tech empires also inspire majority world policies in ways that ultimately reproduce the very hierarchies they purport to challenge.

7

AI futures reconsidered

In this book, we have approached AITs not as isolated technological inventions determining societal transformations, but as expressions of the unequal, conflict-ridden and contradictory economic, political and social conditions under which they are devised and diffused. What do the perspective and analysis we have offered in this book suggest for the road ahead? In this final chapter, we consider two angles: ex ante, the direction of technological development and how it changes our economies and societies is open. Innovation does not follow a predetermined path and depending on the direction in which we push, with our money and politics, we could end up in very different places. We therefore first explore to what degree present-day alternative approaches (including open source AI, federated learning or edge AI) might offer fundamentally different trajectories. And second, we revisit the potential of bottom-up resistance against techno-political developments that people experience as undesirable or harmful. How much scope is there for workers, citizens or even smaller countries to push back against a version of the digital future that, at least for some people, makes things worse rather than better? As we have shown, the map of who wins and who loses is chequered in both rich and poor economies. What does that imply for the chances of taking back a modicum of control in emerging tech?

Tying it all together in the final section, we return to where we began – our four premises: public authorities and institutions matter; the stories we tell about AI may be distorted but have potent effects; geopolitics always hovers in the background; and global inequalities and asymmetries are features, not bugs, of AI transformations. Throughout this book, we employed these lenses to explore how we came to the present moment of a perceived global AI transformation. What do they suggest for what might lie ahead?

Profit-driven tech transformations and their discontents

Despite its ring of novelty, much of AI's impact on the global political economy follows an old, familiar script. For all the buzz about radical disruption – pledges to reinvent production processes or replace much of knowledge work – the real engine behind today's AI boom is simple: the promise of profit. Strip away the hype and you are left with a speculative money game driven by breathless hopes of future riches. Startups around the world race to launch LLMs built on massive, often legally dubious data grabs and unsustainable energy waste. Tech giants leverage enormous resources to tighten their grip on the digital economy. AI adoption varies across industries and regions, but most often the focus remains on marginal cost-cutting and pilot projects. Venture capital hunts for the next unicorn, seeking to capitalize early on projected fortunes. Governments try to score political points among their constituencies by backing innovation with minimal guardrails in geopolitical jostles over economic competitiveness. On every level, commercial incentives shape not just how AI is developed and deployed, but where, by whom, and towards which ends.

As a cluster of technologies with very diverse functions and market dynamics, AI is powerful and, in many cases, genuinely innovative. We wrote this book because we, too, believe something transformative may be going on. As we discussed in Chapter 2, AITs have the potential to reshape business, politics and everyday life, albeit unevenly and to varying degrees depending on socio-economic context and geography. But the crux is that their path ahead is not steered mainly by what these technologies could do, technically speaking, but rather by what those in charge and owning them want them to do.

If we accept for a moment that AI were to generate colossal economic value in the coming decades, that value could help redress inequality and widespread poverty, help finance the fight against climate breakdown and tackle other major global challenges. A recent calculation has it that AI-generated value and wealth is estimated to be $25 trillion and eradicating global poverty would cost around $175 billion per year for a period of 25 years: on paper, AI could indeed "solve world poverty five times over".[1] But how realistic is that, given that AI is overwhelmingly shaped by entrenched business interests? At stake is a simple but profound question: is AI evolving primarily in line with its technological promises or mostly shaped by well-known economic logics? The AI matrix, entangling tech development in a web of profits, power and politics, makes us sceptical.

This section integrates our earlier reflections on how the global AI boom is less about breaking with the past than reinforcing it. Competitive advantage in AI today hinges on proprietary control of capital and key infrastructures, data hoarding and economies of scale, all of which favour the biggest players, who usually steer things from the Northern hemisphere. The current "AI trans-formation" is not a rupture from capitalism, but its evolution, motivated less by projections of techno-utopia or dystopia than by the system's enduring dynamics. We realize, of course, that private startups need capital to grow, and that those who provide it are in it for the economic returns. In that sense, we are pointing out the obvious. That is necessary, however, because so much AI debate keeps ignoring just how driven the whole development is by a very specific economic logic, one that that prioritizes self-interest over the com-mon good, short-term success over long-term impact and material gains over intangible ones. Capitalism is the elephant in AI's engine room.

At its core, the post-ChatGPT AI boom is built on entrenched infrastruc-tures of accumulation: opaque datasets, often scraped from copyrighted mate-rial and social media, large-scale computing power, platform ecosystems that lock users in, invisible and precarious data labour and a flood of speculative capital in search of the next big payoff. The weight of these factors varies with the specific type of AIT. Still, a handful of well-financed startups and transna-tional firms dominate the development of leading AI applications, especially in typically capital-intensive areas like generative AI. These companies are best positioned to absorb the costs of model training – whether by building pro-prietary systems in-house or acquiring promising startups before they become serious competition – while externalizing the associated risks onto the public at large. As we argued in Chapter 3, the result is an AI landscape driven less by open innovation than by market concentration, consolidation of power and resources and the deep pockets of those already at the top.

AI, in short, is shaped by logics of control, enclosure and scale. These forces dictate not only which technologies get built, but which applications are prioritized and promoted and who stands to gain the most. Building more general-purpose AITs is attractive for Alphabet not just because of technical versatility and capacities, but also because the firm can embed them across different business functions and industries, offered as software-as-a-service and predictably monetized through subscriptions. The quest for profit also motivates the new forms of enclosure we see behind many headline-grabbing AITs. OpenAI's top-performing models, for instance, have been closed-source for years. Deploying AITs often comes with strings attached, such as tying users into cloud ecosystems like AWS or Microsoft Azure.

The result is an AI sector defined by winner-takes-most dynamics across many application areas. Those with competitive advantages in computing, data, capital or expert staff are in a superior position to shape how the tech evolves and how it is used. This sets off a reinforcing cycle: dominant players develop or adopt stronger models, attract more users and investment, gen-erate more data and feedback, and widen their lead over competitors. In this scenario, technical performance and economic scale are inseparable. And even when new AI-native firms emerge, they typically slot into digital value chains already dominated by Big Tech – whether through infrastructure dependencies, funding ties or pathways to M&A. The shape of today's AI transformations is not just a story about tech, but also a reflection of the structural logic of advanced capitalism.

But it does not have to stay that way. Big Tech dominance does not mean that there are no alternatives that push back against monopolistic tendencies, though such alternatives may be small in scale. Open source projects, more lightweight and task-specific models or decentralized approaches suggest potential paths beyond today's dominant business models. Even here, the gravitational pull of profit-seeking is often hard to escape given the competitive and financing constraints. Such initiatives deserve recognition and potential support but also critical scrutiny. Volunteer-led projects often run on digital infrastructure owned by the very firms they are supposed to bypass. Meanwhile, public sector and civil society efforts face meaningful barriers: chronic underfunding, limited access to computing resources and relevant data, and a shortage of skilled developers – indispensable inputs for creating viable alternatives to dominant AI applications. And Big Tech has so far proven remarkably adept at outmanoeuvring or even absorbing challenges to its power.[2] The technological seeds of a different AI future may exist, but they grow in soil still owned by the incumbents.

One of the most widely discussed counter currents – particularly since DeepSeek shook the AI market in early 2025 – is the open source AI movement. Rising in response to the opacity and concentration of proprietary systems, open source aims to democratize access by making training data, model weights, code or interfaces freely available for public use, inspection and modification. Motivations behind open-sourcing AITs vary. Some are rooted in ideals of transparency and accountability. Some want to "hack capitalism" at its core rather than merely tinkering with its symptoms.[3] Others are more pragmatic, driven by economic gain – Meta's open source initiatives, for example, can hardly count as altruistic. Still, the open source movement has made significant inroads even in resource-intensive fields like LLMs. Stanford researchers note that nearly two-thirds of foundation models released in 2023 were open source.[4] Models like EleutherAI's GPT-J and platforms such as Hugging Face have lowered adoption barriers for AI-curious firms and researchers. Public datasets allow model training without breaching copyright and open source cloud infrastructure (think of OpenStack or Kubernetes) gives developers more control and flexibility when deploying AITs, compared to working within Big Tech's walled gardens.

Open source ecosystems also create space for developing AI collaboratively. Volunteers contribute code, bug fixes and performance enhancements, which can enable more distributed and adaptive innovation. This peer-driven model fosters accountability between developers and users and allows resource-strapped research labs, non-profits and smaller businesses to shape AI on their own terms, often beyond the pressures of immediate profit-making.

In practice, however, open source remains limited. As discussed in Chapter 3, many models are only partially open. Meta's Llama, for example, has open model weights but withholds details about its training data, making full reproduction of the model or a thorough audit impossible. This kind of "open-washing" creates the appearance of transparency while preserving control over some of the most critical AI components. More troubling still, many power-ful open source AITs ultimately rely on infrastructure, cloud credits or tech support from the very corporate giants they suggest sidestepping. Volunteer labour can end up reinforcing the dominance of firms like Meta, which inte-grates open source innovations into proprietary profit-driven applications on its social media platforms. Here, collaboration ends up reinforcing Big Tech's competitive edge – never mind the highfalutin openness rhetoric.

Another way to lower AI adoption barriers is through smaller, more effi-cient models. Designed for narrow tasks or optimized for reduced resource use, these are very different beasts to foundation models. Some are "distilla-tions" of bigger models, replicating LLM performance while drastically reduc-ing size.[5] Others are purpose-built to minimize size or costs. Such models suffice for many real-world applications. For instance, credit agency Experian replaced its general-purpose chatbot with a smaller in-house model trained on company-specific data to cut costs without sacrificing performance.[6] After all, why would you need a model trained on everything from Nepal's history to nuclear thermodynamics to answer customer questions about credit scores? The rhetorical focus on "general-purpose" models, beyond being a marketing device towards investors, might well miss the point of specialization as a key achievement of human knowledge generation and product development.

Smaller models are well-suited for environments with limited data, strict privacy requirements or severe energy constraints. They may offer entry options for local tech consultancies and resellers and thus generate value and jobs further away from the global centres of model development. Their relative simplicity can make them easier and cheaper to integrate with local informa-tion systems, allowing new players to deploy AITs independently of propri-etary application processing interfaces or the cloud. Consider, for example, the rise of "frugal AI", in which practical utility takes precedence over sheer scale without compromising efficiency.[7] These models, too, are not without their constraints. They can be less flexible, require substantial customization for each separate case and struggle with more complex tasks. And although they are smaller in size, their development and deployment still require technical expertise, infrastructures and context-sensitive data, resources that remain unevenly distributed.

Efforts to decentralize AI training and inference through distributed training, federated learning and edge AI also contest the dominance of centralized cloud infrastructures. Distributed training splits workloads across multiple devices, whereas federated learning allows several servers to train models together without even exchanging any raw data. Edge AI, meanwhile, helps process data locally on devices like smartphones or Internet of Things hardware, which cuts down response time and limits dependence on remote servers. These approaches are particularly valuable in highly regulated sectors such as healthcare where data privacy and security are paramount, but also in regions with limited internet connectivity. Keeping computation closer to data's point of origin, they enable faster and more responsive applications, which can also support more environmentally sustainable AI systems. This offers a different vision of AI infrastructure: small scale, locally embedded, less extractive.

Decentralization has its own limits. The hardware ecosystems supporting them (smartphones, operating systems and networking gear) are themselves controlled by a few tech behemoths like Apple, Nvidia or Alphabet. Edge devices' computing capacity constrains the complexity of models they can run. Federated learning depends on stable network connectivity and is vulnerable to model poisoning attacks.[8] Often, these limitations are not dealbreakers, as most users do not try to simulate climate systems or generate architectural blueprints on an old smartphone. The broader point still stands, however: whereas decentralized approaches may reduce dependencies on cloud providers, they do not break free from the deeper concentration of infrastructural resources. And they do not necessarily escape the profit logic. In fact, some tech giants are already adapting. Apple, for example, has incorporated edge AI principles into its Apple Intelligence system, showing how decentralization can be coopted into existing power structures as a competitive advantage – and as a golden opportunity to sell new hardware, in this case powerful iPhones that can run AI models locally.

Taken together, these alternative models (open source, more frugal and decentralized) mark genuine technical departures from the dominant path of AI development. They propose more sustainable, pluralistic and context-sensitive approaches to building and using AI, and they surely deserve recognition for doing so. But technical differences alone are not enough to deliver structural change. Each of these models operates within broader socioeconomic constraints: capital flows, infrastructural bottlenecks and global asymmetries of power. Without more fundamental shifts, even the most well-intentioned alternatives can end up reproducing the dynamics they originally hoped to disrupt. As we have argued throughout, innovation never happens in a vacuum. At present, it is largely shaped by the logics of capital accumulation, market concentration and first-mover advantages, and these, in turn, are structured by the opportunities and constraints which regulation and policy-making set. Promising alternatives are frequently absorbed into the strategies of incumbent powers – repurposed, rebranded and left ultimately toothless.

As long as AI development is driven by hype, profit motives, and private control over data and infrastructure – all within a global landscape rife with geopolitical rivalry and structural inequalities – its transformative promise remains bound to the prevailing hierarchies of capital and power. Bringing in a more democratic, equitable, and sustainable AI future takes more than some safeguards, tech fixes or smart regulation. Unless the underlying structures and power relations are part of a different vision of AI in our societies, we risk reproducing the very injustices these technologies could help overcome.

Pockets of resistance and what we might learn from them

The future impact of AITs on political-economic relations across the globe also hinges on the relative force of resistance and alternatives. Counter-actions and -narratives might tackle any of the problematic dynamics we have described in this book: regulation and taxation could curb dominant business models of big AI firms. Community-owned or public infrastructures could be alternatives to proprietary ones. Labour law could push back against the mantra of labour productivity boosts in sectoral AI uses and workplace monitoring devices. Novel forms of data sharing compensation could counter exploitative data skimming. Local and co-op tech development could attenuate colonial and imperial relationships in global tech diffusion. And more prominent conversations about the dark sides of AI innovation in the shadow of geopolitical competition could help hold governments to account for their AI policies.

At present, there is no major resistance movement ready to roll out a more equitable AI development at large. Still, we consider smaller pockets of resistance as meaningful pointers towards progressive change in the global political economy of AI. If nothing else, existing initiatives which counter a profit-driven and highly unequal AI diffusion show how the contemporary distribution of AI-related costs and benefits remains a deeply political choice. They facilitate discussions about desirable and walkable paths to fairer and more sustainable AI futures. To gauge ways forward in that cautious yet hopeful manner, let us illustrate initiatives and countermovements at two levels: the hyper-concentrated infrastructural power of Big Tech and AI empires, and the squeeze on labour and workers' rights under a banner of "AI productivity gains".

On their own, open source initiatives cannot tackle adverse market concentration. Individual developers' or labs' use of open source to gain competitive advantages clashes fundamentally with a community-oriented interpretation of collaborative and inclusive software development; it also conflicts with an environmental framing that highlights how collaborative open source development could save scarce planetary resources such as electricity and water.[9] Critics fear that powerful AI incumbents mainly mobilize discourses of "openness" to bolster their market positions, pre-empt restrictive regulation, set AI development standards and exploit the free labour of open source developers.[10] Without close scrutiny of what is meant and practiced under the open source heading and by whom, and without also addressing ownership or at least regulating access to utilities such as databases and cloud computing, we will not overcome the abuse of market dominance and its adverse societal effects.

Several projects do try to provide alternative LLMs, if not realistically to challenge US and Chinese dominance then at least to provide locally competitive and culturally aligned options. Their rationales range from boosting local competitiveness – without questioning profit-oriented AI markets as such – to community-owned non-profit solutions for promoting minority languages and culture. While many such initiatives are coated in socially-progressive rhetoric of diverse and pluralist AI, some still play to the tune of profit-making (understandably so). Projects that embrace genuine non-profit alternatives are more utopian than modest calls for a diversified global AI market, breaking oligopolies and distributing profits more equally. That, after all, would be an achievement in itself. And yet, more radical resistance movements raise the nagging normative question whether AI development based on our collective heritage (human language and culture, for example) should be enclosed as private property for rent-seeking purposes in the first place.

At the more profit-driven end of the spectrum, the Singaporean state and research institutions invest around $52 million to build their own multilingual LLM.[11] While partly advertised as a decolonization project which can lower the dependency on US-developed LLMs, which misrepresent local idioms and cultural practices, the project speaks mainly to Singapore's global tech ambitions. Government policies echo the AI race theme we discussed in Chapter 6, with the Singaporean LLM surfacing as a "national effort" that demonstrates a "commitment to become a global AI hub".[12] It met with unexpected resistance from local writers, who worry about the model's for-profit use beyond initial research and public services and a lack of compensation for use of their content in model training. Such initiatives can diversify global AI markets and reduce dependency on the US and China. It is less clear that they benefit any local data annotator or public service recipient as long as narrowly conceived productivity and labour cost savings remain the core.

Closer towards the decolonial activism end of the spectrum we find initiatives such as Masakhane's facilitation of knowledge exchange and collaborative development of natural language processing tech in African languages. Here, the resistance against a marginalization of several thousand local languages is directly linked to a critique of insufficient funding for natural language processing projects in non-colonial languages and the obstacles to home-grown African AI solutions. Another example is the Kenyan-based non-profit Amref Health Africa, which partnered with researchers from the University of Southern California and Microsoft's AI for Good Lab to develop a model that forecasts malnutrition using anonymized health data and complementary inputs such as satellite images from the Kenyan Ministry of Health.[13] While the model runs on Microsoft Azure, its aim is to equip community health organizations with actionable insights. Another project, called *Indigenous AI*, is even further removed from any economic competitiveness rationale: since 2019, it has brought together communities across the globe in workshops to write an "Indigenous Protocol on AI" that charts alternative epistemologies for global AI development, including different framings of tech's legitimate role in society and its effects on non-humans and the natural habitat.[14]

Other initiatives acknowledge that neither a local LLM nor a competitive AI application (think of DataProphet's manufacturing optimization tools) and not even a successful tech cluster in the Global South (like Kenya's Silicon Savannah) will dethrone the Chinese and American AI leaders. Not unless there was also very serious investment – financially but also in terms of skills and industrial policy – in computing power in the majority world. One valiant attempt is Galaxy Backbone, a Nigerian startup that helps the government and private customers become more independent from AWS, Microsoft Azure and Google Cloud.[15] Again, this endeavour operates *within* a capitalist logic, seeking to carve out a regionally competitive niche rather than a non-profit alternative as such.

But even then, with a few data centres around Lagos, Galaxy Backbone surely cannot take on the global incumbents alone. The contours of a more decentralized approach to cloud – with many similar local providers cutting out small market shares from Big Tech – emerges as we write, especially as countries increasingly worry about their digital sovereignty. In Europe, governments start to opt for open source software solutions to decrease vendor lock-in. The German state of Schleswig-Holstein decided to stop working with Microsoft during the Biden administration and to move to LibreOffice for its 30,000 state employees.[16] The municipality of Copenhagen announced similar ambitions. And Amsterdam, too, is hatching a strategy to decrease its dependence on US Big Tech.[17] A key question for the future is to what extent such a decentral countering of infrastructural hegemony needs orchestration and collective action of governments and regional blocs. And to what degree could a Eurostack wean the EU of dependence on foreign tech without copying oligopolistic business models that would once more suffocate local players and communities who want to benefit from AI on their own terms?

A second line of resistance in AI-transformed economies comes from labour movements, broadly speaking. From their perspective, it seems doubtful that securing good living standards, economic democracy and social cohesion all hinge on success in a putative AI race, certainly in those places and sectors that have no chance of "winning" such a race in the first place. Instead, they hope to safeguard the wealth and welfare that countries have already, and to ensure their fair distribution. We have the technology to feed and sustain the planet and its inhabitants already. A lack of AI is not a bottleneck. Rather than simply accepting that a global AI race requires urgent state action and investment, critics could ask an alternative question around which to mobilize: how can the (human-made) AI tech boom serve societies in achieving a fairer distribution of wealth and life chances as well as wider democratic participation? The visions of the global techno-optimist left (a marginal standpoint in left-leaning organizations at best) point in that very direction: accelerationists on the left "embrace the logistical organisation of the most exploitative business on the planet" and dream of a future in which tech helps set workers free from strenuous labour and the inequalities stemming from capital-labour relations.[18] This future – although intriguing – looks rather unlikely.

Where AI innovations constitute another opportunity for capital owners to increase profitability and to economize on wages for the remaining hands operating the cogs in the machine, the effective protection of workers' rights, pay and social benefits emerges as key battlefield. Think of the well-paid lab workers who cleaned data and trained the first models and how, through splicing this work into tiny, platform-managed gigs, a small army of poorly paid annotators emerged. In 2023, Kenyan content moderators openly contested draining working conditions and unfair pay of as little as $2 an hour to make OpenAI's models "less toxic".[19] Or consider the first unionized labour movement at Amazon US (the Amazon Labor Union) founded in New York in 2022 against fierce opposition by the company. It fights for "a living wage with fair pay increases; safer working conditions to prevent injuries and fatalities; job security and protection from arbitrary firings; dignity and respect for all employees".[20] The Amazon union also exemplifies how to make labour's voice audible against powerful and hard-nosed management, including through strikes.

Some fierce labour activists faced with AI tech rollouts in their workplaces have started sabotaging and playing such technologies to counter usage that seeks to replace or control labour, from Amazon warehouse workers collectively manipulating their productivity figures to office workers using software that feigns desk activity to fool tracking software. For Gavin Mueller such forms of activism stand in the tradition of an older "high-tech luddite" movement for which the struggle over free software was a means to challenge proprietary business models while "[preserving] independent and craft-like working conditions for programmers".[21]

Labour movements also call for tighter regulation of new AI-enabled practices, such as automated recruitment and surveillance.[22] Basketball players pressured the US National Basketball Association to restrict clubs' use of automatically gathered player performance data in salary negotiations.[23] Gojek ride hailing workers in Jakarta, Indonesia, formed "base camps" across the city to stay informed about workplace developments, help each other out and stay safe, develop communication and policy strategies towards the platform and government, and also share and scale workarounds of the algorithmic performance trackers that squeeze job autonomy and penalize them for illness.[24]

It is unlikely that workers everywhere can match basketball stars' bargaining power. In fact, as a general trend, AI diffusion dents worker solidarity instead of buttressing it. In Chapter 5 we argued that where AI is used to boost productivity and continuously monitor employees, the association of workers and their identification with each other tends to fizzle out. Exploitation and labour optimization remain present. But algorithmic management depersonalizes and atomizes work, making it even harder than before for workers (and consumers) to identify others as class allies. Just as the dichotomy between paid labour and capitalists in industrialism replaced the central antagonism between landowners and tenants in feudal societies, new divisions emerge between the dataset owners on one hand and most people on the other who are either mere data providers, constantly monitored in their behaviour, who feature as highly exploitable data workers or as entirely unpaid "freemium" data-producing consumers and users.

This fragmentation of collective identities also emerges from the ambivalent relationship many individuals have with digital technologies. We often combine experiences of stress, anxiety and loss of control with intense use of AITs themselves, whether at home or through the manifold apps that leverage them. Notwithstanding warnings about AI's potential for harm, many people feel that they profit from AITs in their personal lives and use them enthusiastically. This ambiguity obstructs a more articulated political position towards them. Worries about discrimination and privacy violations apart, the lack of transparency about how, why and to whose benefit data is gathered makes collective identity formation and political mobilization against data appropriation and rent extraction cumbersome.

Some labour voices tackle the systemic question of capitalist accumulation through AI tech on the back of both workers and consumer-users of digital tech. Antônio Lisboa, Secretary for International Relations at the Brazilian Trade Union Association, recently used the Brazilian G20 presidency to warn political leaders that AITs would merely serve "to concentrate geopolitical, economic and financial power" unless workers everywhere have an institutionalized say in AI adoption in their workplaces.[25] Danish social partners have been successful not only in co-determining working conditions in the platform economy, but also in the "use of AI and algorithmic management when new technologies are introduced at company level".[26] Then again, Denmark is Denmark, and such examples will be hard to copy elsewhere.

The diffusion of AITs tends to weaken the working class as a collective force in politics. It also dilutes more local group identities. At the same time, it is unclear how crosscutting identities, say of a new global precariat uniting with social media users and smallholder farmers exposed to "digital intrusion", could become a source for political mobilization. Their spatial scattering, different identities, and precarity suggests a low mobilization potential and weak power resources, especially when facing the much more concentrated political-economic power of Big Tech and societal groups who are net beneficiaries of current tech diffusion. So how much scope is there for new forms of national, let alone global, mobilization or engagement around its political-economic impact? We wonder whether the institutions created thanks to the struggles over labour rights and social policies in the twentieth century (at least in the Global North) are still fit for countering the adverse effects of AI. As societies, we should pursue the discussion of feasible "new modalities of counterpolitics" to balance out competing interests over the direction of AI transformations with urgency.[27]

Thinking about AI futures through a global political economy lens

We opened this book with a plea for a political economy perspective on AI, proposing four analytical lenses. First, public policy shapes how, when and where AI is made and how it is diffused. Politics also mediates the effects of AI, whether on labour markets or wealth inequality. Any account of "the economic impact of AI" is incomplete without considering how politics and policy are implicated in what happens. Second, the decisions that both governments and companies take about AI are driven by speculative narratives about the future. AI is shaped by what people with money and influence think about it. Third, this plays out in a climate of an intense geoeconomic "race to AI" especially between the US and China, with the EU as a distant third. This competition feeds government perspectives and perceptions of urgency. And fourth, all this unfolds in a strati-fied and highly unequal global political economy. A bifurcated discussion that portrays AI either as a wealth booster for all or as an inequality engine ignores just how uneven AI's socio-economic effects are across countries, economic sec-tors, workplaces or regions. What do these propositions imply for the road ahead?

The shape of the future digital economy will depend on governments' pol-itical will and capacity to steer it. As we outlined in Chapter 6, many countries already have (or will end up with) significant digital dependencies. We iden-tified imperial dynamics at play, with the US and China especially vying for dominance in different places. Some countries, such as those in the EU, India, Russia, the UK, UAE, Japan and South Korea, stand little chance of becoming digital imperial powers themselves, but they are powerful enough to create niches for domestic firms and at least steer digitization (and hence AI policy) within their own borders. Many others have little choice but to either accept or refuse what China or the US offer them because the backbone of digital infra-structures will be built and governed from there. In other words, the capacity to steer digital futures is a function of digital sovereignty. The less control a country has over its tech stack, the costlier a policy that departs from dominant industry trajectories will be. This explains the current geopolitical struggle over tech regulation and development, and we expect it to intensify further.

Even where digital sovereignty is greater, the result is no simple AI volun-tarism. Governing AI is difficult. AITs evolve quickly, are broadly applicable, making the operationalization and enforcement of abstract governance prin-ciples challenging. Outlawing discriminatory AI on paper is much easier than enforcing the rules. The practical difficulties of translating political ambitions into action complicate AI governance. And they highlight its transversal char-acter: AI policy broadly conceived includes taxation policies, public support for research and development, potential protectionism, education policy, and so on. Insisting that political institutions and decisions matter is not the same as claiming that a desirable AI future could simply be willed into action.

Indeed, the complexity of such political steering provides arguments against it: it is simply very difficult to get right. How much easier to follow the neo-liberal and deregulatory impulse and simply let things play out – even if that means abdicating democratic responsibility and letting the already powerful have their way. Effective public policy is not impossible. But because it is a lot harder than imposing import tariffs or adjusting tax rates, it will take prow-ess and determination to make it work. For politicians and policymakers, the path of least resistance and risk remains appealing, stacking the odds against coordinated changes of direction.

Even when there is domestic political capacity to steer AITs, it is a question of political will whether and in which direction it will be used. We expect a potential push away from the current drift of things (for most countries this means domination by US or Chinese tech) to stem from four potential sources. The first would involve local firms eager to get a larger share of the digital pie pushing for protectionism. While plausible in principle, no country hosts domestic AI companies strong enough to mount a successful challenge against digital openness. Although tech companies in Europe or India might champion digital protectionism, they typically lack political clout, unlike German car makers or French wine producers. Second, governments of rich countries see AI as a potential anchor for future national economic development and push local initiatives for that reason. The Gulf States come to mind here, but these examples are specific because of their exceptional wealth derived from natural resources. Third, governments may identify AI dependence as a security vulnerability, effectively resisting the imperial dynamics that we outlined above. Here, the EU and India are prime candidates, even if it remains an open question whether they can muster the political unity and will to implement comprehensive alternatives to foreign tech. And finally, governments may feel pressure from below (from citizens and workers) to chart a digital course that departs from the current direction of travel. As we just outlined, however, AI politics has fractured class relations rather than solidified them. They are not an easy topic around which people can coalesce. While as citizens we believe that more forceful bottom-up interventions would be warranted, the analysts among us remain sceptical as to how easily they can be achieved.

That said, change could come from a very different direction: throughout, we have highlighted the hype that has pushed resource-intensive AITs such as LLMs. We remain unconvinced that they will live up to the disproportional promises that surround them. Remarkable AI breakthroughs do not mean that our economies will be unrecognizable two or three decades hence. For better or worse, they will look much more like they do today than techno-optimists or doomsayers predict. In short, the AI bubble may burst. In the immediate years after the global financial crisis, hardly anyone was talking about AI as the next big thing. Now it is everywhere. Economic trends and emergencies have followed each other with astonishing speed during the past two decades. It is hard to imagine right now, but sooner or later something else will grab the attention of policymakers and dominate speculation about our economic future. Already, rearmament and the race over satellite technology in the face of geopolitical tensions absorbs immense public resources. Grenades top graphics processing units on most governments' shopping lists.

What could be next? A dramatic, even if localized, climate catastrophe – as in Kim Stanley Robinson's *The Ministry for the Future* – could refocus minds.[28] Donald Trump's policies might trigger a dollar collapse, with trade disruption and economic recessions making huge capital expenditures on AI seem an unaffordable luxury. Artificial general intelligence might materialize, shaking up much conventional thinking about AI and economic affairs. Or might another hype cycle, focused on another technology, sap enthusiasm and excitement away from AI?

We do not know where things are going, in particular with something like artificial general intelligence. What is clear, however, is that history does not progress in a straight line and that public and political attention can shift abruptly. Given that hopes and fears themselves drive AI policies to a great extent, a shifting narrative might usher in another unexpected shift in AI's role in the economy. We have warned against the temptation to see the future as little more than extrapolated current trends. That applies here, too. That makes it even more important to assess not only what AI can do technically, but also what it is imagined to do and how these imaginaries are mobilized. Whether utopian or nightmarish, such narratives are used to justify major institutional and organizational changes well ahead of any evidence of actual capability or public debate. Keeping a close eye on the labour market effects of AI adoption and involving workers in decisions about tech diffusion is key not just for labour relations themselves, but for humanity as a whole, at least if we see work as a meaningful social relation that is central to people's lives.

For the moment, the bipolar competition between the US as declining hegemon and China as potent challenger seems unlikely to wane. Neither power would accept voluntary subordination to the other. Even without belligerent rhetoric and trade wars, AI competition would remain a fact. The geopolitical wildcard to our mind is not a substantial easing of the competition, but rather its violent escalation. Meanwhile, China and the US will push ahead with AI development. Slowing it down in the name of mitigating the societal consequences or limiting potential harms is anathema to the current race dynamics. And even where regulation exists – as with China's rules on permissible AI use – it seems unrealistic to expect meaningful constraints on the power of homegrown tech giants. By the same token, given their mutual suspicion, it is hard to imagine global cooperation in AI governance involving both countries.

For the time being, the dynamics in and between these two countries will have a disproportional influence on AI development and diffusion, and the effects will be varied and felt across the world. AITs have both integrating and differentiating effects in the global political economy. Like other digital technologies, they bring together what happens in different places through the connections they establish or facilitate. That is true for finance and trade (especially services trade) but also for data analysis and the remote provision of data annotation. Large tech companies build cross-border dependencies into digital ecosystems that customers struggle to shake off. Production chains for tech hardware are extremely complex and hard to reconfigure. At the same time, because digital products can easily be made at scale and delivered remotely, they are controlled from afar, even when the data that feeds them as raw material is produced locally.

As political economists, we see "the economy" as thoroughly suffused with politics. Economic institutions, laws, trade policies are all products of struggles among competing interests and visions. This also means that AI's future, and the way it affects us all, is not predetermined. Societies are full of contradictions and tensions, countermovements and resistance to the status quo. The short-term future is unknown. While it is reasonable to argue that some political economy dynamics are more deeply entrenched than the current AI hype suggests, the unfolding of both crises and resistance also means that the scope for unexpected twists and turns in the story of AITs is substantial. At the very least, then, we hope to contribute a heuristic for thinking about the global political economy of AI, fully aware that future diagnoses of its transformative potential will require new judgement calls. The future remains open – and to our mind, that is a good thing.

Notes

Chapter 1: Beyond the hype: a global political economy view of AI

1 Marc Andreesen, "Why AI will save the world", 6 June 2023, pmarca.substack.com: last accessed 29 August 2025.
2 Joe Biden, Presidential farewell speech, 15 January 2025, transcript on: bidenwhitehouse. archives.gov: last accessed 17 March 2025.
3 Kevin Scott and Greg Shaw, *Reprogramming the American Dream: From Rural America to Silicon Valley: Making AI Serve Us All* (London: HarperCollins, 2020).
4 In the order mentioned, the reports are: Alex Singla *et al.*, *The State of AI in Early 2024* (McKinsey, 2024); PwC, "Sizing the Prize", 2017, www.pwc.com/gx/en/issues/analytics/ assets/pwc-ai-analysis-sizing-the-prize-report.pdf: last accessed 9 September 2025; Michael Chui *et al.*, *The Economic Potential of Generative AI: The next Productivity Frontier* (McKinsey, 2023).
5 European Commission, *Fostering a European Approach to Artificial Intelligence* (2021), 4, www.digital-strategy.ec.europa.eu/en/library/coordinated-plan-artificial-intelligence-2021-review.
6 The Economist, "Yuval Noah Harari and Mustafa Suleyman on the Future of AI". *The Economist*, 14 September 2023, https://www.economist.com/films/2023/09/14/yuval-noah-harari-and-mustafa-suleyman-on-the-future-of-ai.
7 Toby Ord, *The Precipice: Existential Risk and the Future of Humanity* (London: Bloomsbury, 2021); Nick Bostrom, *Superintelligence: Paths, Dangers, Strategies* (Oxford: Oxford University Press, 2014); Yoshua Bengio, "AI and catastrophic risk", *Journal of Democracy* 34:4 (2023), 111–21.
8 Yarden Katz, *Artificial Whiteness: Politics and Ideology in Artificial Intelligence* (New York: Columbia University Press, 2020); Catherine D'Ignazio and Lauren F. Klein, *Data Feminism* (Cambridge, MA: MIT Press, 2020).
9 Shoshana Zuboff, *The Age of Surveillance Capitalism: The Fight for a Human Future at the New Frontier of Power* (New York: PublicAffairs, 2019).
10 Ted Chiang, "Will A.I. become the new McKinsey?", *The New Yorker*, 4 May 2023.
11 Cathy O'Neil, *Weapons of Math Destruction: How Big Data Increases Inequality and Threatens Democracy* (London: Crown, 2016), 13.
12 Virginia Eubanks, *Automating Inequality: How High-Tech Tools Profile, Police, and Punish the Poor* (New York: St Martin's Press, 2018).
13 James Bridle, *New Dark Age: Technology and the End of the Future* (London: Verso, 2023), 9.
14 Samantha Murphy Kelly, "Elon Musk says AI will take all our jobs", CNN, 23 May 2024.

15 Attilio Di Battista *et al.*, *The Future of Jobs Report 2023* (WEF, 2023), 6.
16 Neda Atanasoski and Kalindi Vora, *Surrogate Humanity: Race, Robots, and the Politics of Technological Futures* (Durham, NC: Duke University Press, 2019).
17 Nick Dyer-Witheford *et al.*, *Inhuman Power: Artificial Intelligence and the Future of Capitalism* (London: Pluto, 2019), 145.
18 Bruno Latour, "When things strike back: a possible contribution of 'Science Studies' to the social sciences", *British Journal of Sociology* 51:1 (2000), 107–23.
19 Julie E. Cohen, "The biopolitical public domain: the legal construction of the surveillance economy", *Philosophy & Technology* 31:2 (2018), 213–33; Katharina Pistor, *The Code of Capital: How the Law Creates Wealth and Inequality* (Princeton, NJ: Princeton University Press, 2019).
20 Emily M. Bender *et al.*, "On the dangers of stochastic parrots: can language models be too big? 🦜", *Proceedings of the 2021 ACM Conference on Fairness, Accountability, and Transparency*, ACM, 3 March 2021, 610–23.
21 Daron Acemoglu and Simon Johnson, *Power and Progress: Our Thousand-Year Struggle Over Technology and Prosperity* (New York: PublicAffairs, 2023).
22 Matteo Pasquinelli, *The Eye of the Master: A Social History of Artificial Intelligence* (London: Verso, 2023).
23 Robert Boyer, "Platform capitalism: a socio-economic analysis", *Socio-Economic Review* 20:4 (2022), 1870ff, 1877.
24 K. Sabeel Rahman and Kathleen Thelen, "The rise of the platform business model and the transformation of twenty-first-century capitalism", *Politics & Society* 47:2 (2019), 177–204.
25 Evgeny Morozov, *To Save Everything, Click Here: The Folly of Technological Solutionism* (New York: PublicAffairs, 2014).
26 Adrian Daub, *What Tech Calls Thinking: An Inquiry into the Intellectual Bedrock of Silicon Valley* (New York: FSG, 2020).
27 Joachim Haupt, "Facebook futures: Mark Zuckerberg's discursive construction of a better world", *New Media & Society* 23:2 (2021), 237–57.
28 Douglas Rushkoff, *Survival of the Richest: Escape Fantasies of the Tech Billionaires* (New York: Norton, 2022).
29 Judith Clifton *et al.*, "When machines think for us: the consequences for work and place", *Cambridge Journal of Regions, Economy and Society* 13:1 (2020), 13.
30 Jascha Bareis *et al.*, "Technology hype: dealing with bold expectations and overpromising", *TATuP – Zeitschrift Für Technikfolgenabschätzung in Theorie und Praxis* 32:3 (2023), 12.
31 Ngai-Ling Sum and Bob Jessop, *Towards a Cultural Political Economy: Putting Culture in Its Place in Political Economy* (Cheltenham: Elgar, 2013).
32 Jens Beckert, *Imagined Futures: Fictional Expectations and Capitalist Dynamics* (Cambridge, MA: Harvard University Press, 2016).
33 See www.cac.gov.cn/2023-10/18/c_1699291032884978.htm; Adam Satariano and Paul Mozur, "'To the future': Saudi Arabia spends big to become an A.I. superpower", *The New York Times*, 25 April 2024.
34 J. Bareis and C. Katzenbach, "Talking AI into being: the narratives and imaginaries of national AI strategies and their performative politics", *Science, Technology & Human Values* 47:5 (2022), 855–81; Regine Paul, "European AI 'trusted throughout the world': how risk-based regulation fashions a competitive common market for artificial intelligence", *Regulation & Governance* 18:4 (2024), 1065–82.
35 Milan Babić, *Geoökonomie: Anatomie der neuen Weltordnung* (Frankfurt: Suhrkamp, 2025).
36 Tatjana Evas, *European Framework on Ethical Aspects of Artificial Intelligence, Robotics and Related Technologies: European Added Value Assessment* (EPRS, 2020), 22.
37 Troels Krarup and Maja Horst, "European artificial intelligence policy as digital single market making", *Big Data & Society* 10:1 (2023).

38 Mario Draghi, *The Future of European Competitiveness* (Brussels: European Commission, 2024).

39 Mario Damen, *EU Strategic Autonomy 2013–2023: From Concept to Capacity* (EPRS, 2022). See also Daniel Mügge, "EU AI sovereignty: for whom, to what end, and to whose benefit?", *Journal of European Public Policy* 31:8 (2024), 2200–25.

40 National Artificial Intelligence Initiative Act, H.R.6216 (2020), www.congress.gov/bill/116th-congress/house-bill/6216/text: last accessed 28 August 2025; NSCAI, "Final Report by the National Security Commission on AI", 2021,reports.nscai.gov/final-report/introduction: last accessed 28 August 2025.

41 See www.cac.gov.cn/2023-10/18/c_1699291032884978.htm: last accessed 28 August 2025.

42 Paul, "European AI 'trusted throughout the World' ".

43 Anu Bradford, *Digital Empires: The Global Battle to Regulate Technology* (Oxford: Oxford University Press, 2023).

44 Jamie Peck and Rachel Phillips, "The platform conjuncture", *Sociologica* 14:3 (2020), 87.

45 AnnaLee Saxenian, *The New Argonauts: Regional Advantage in a Global Economy* (Cambridge, MA: Harvard University Press, 2006).

46 Florian Butollo, "Digitalization and the geographies of production: towards reshoring or global fragmentation?", *Competition & Change* 25:2 (2021), 259–78.

47 Bradford, *Digital Empires*.

48 Rachel Adams, *The New Empire of AI: The Future of Global Inequality* (Cambridge: Polity, 2024).

49 We follow Adams' description of the majority world as a concept which duly "bears recognition of the fact that the people thus described, despite being politically and economically at the margins of global society, represent the vast majority of the world's population" (*Ibid.*, 16). Adams draws on the conceptualization of Sareeta Amrute *et al.*, *A Primer on AI in/from the Majority World: An Empirical Site and a Standpoint* (Data & Society, 2022).

50 PwC, "PwC's Global Artificial Intelligence Study", 7, figure 2.

51 Adams, *The New Empire of AI*, 8.

52 Jamie Peck, *Variegated Economies* (Oxford: Oxford University Press, 2023).

53 *Ibid.*, 31.

54 Gurminder K. Bhambra, "Colonial global economy: towards a theoretical reorientation of political economy", *Review of International Political Economy* 28:2 (2021), 307–22.

55 Peck, *Variegated Economies*, 220.

Chapter 2: AI's deep roots and many forms

1 See www.betterimagesofai.org: last accessed 28 August 2025.

2 Hussein Abbass, "Editorial: what is artificial intelligence?", *IEEE Transactions on Artificial Intelligence* 2:2 (2021), 94–5.

3 Meredith Broussard, *Artificial Unintelligence: How Computers Misunderstand the World* (Cambridge, MA: MIT Press, 2018), 36.

4 Regine Paul *et al.*, "Introduction", in Regine Paul *et al.* (eds), *Handbook of Public Policy and Artificial Intelligence* (Cheltenham: Elgar, 2024).

5 Bender *et al.*, "On the dangers of stochastic parrots".

6 Melanie Mitchell, *Artificial Intelligence: A Guide for Thinking Humans* (London: Pelican, 2019).

7 Nestor Maslej *et al.*, *Artificial Intelligence Index Report 2024* (Stanford University Institute for Human-Centered AI, 2024), 213ff.

8 Bruce Rogers, "Frans Cronje builds Dataprophet to become foundation for autonomous manufacturing", *Forbes*, 3 August 2022.

9   Kannan Ramaswamy and William Youngdahl, *The Strategic Transformation of John Deere: Precision Agriculture, AI, and the Internet of Things* (Thunderbird School of Global Management, 2023).

10 Sidney Fussell, "Dystopian robot dogs are the latest in a long history of US/Mexico border surveillance", *The Guardian*, 16 February 2022.

11 Steven Feldstein, "The road to digital unfreedom: how artificial intelligence is reshaping repression", *Journal of Democracy* 30:1 (2019), 40–52.

12 Ruha Benjamin, *Race After Technology: Abolitionist Tools for the New Jim Code* (Cambridge: Polity, 2019); Kate Crawford, *Atlas of AI: Power, Politics, and the Planetary Costs of Artificial Intelligence* (New Haven, CT: Yale University Press, 2021).

13 Joy Buolamwini and Timnit Gebru, "Gender shades: intersectional accuracy disparities in commercial gender classification", *Proceedings of Machine Learning Research* 81 (2018), 1–15.

14 Miao Lu and Jack Linchuan Qiu, "Empowerment or warfare? Dark skin, AI camera, and Transsion's patent narratives", *Information, Communication & Society* 25:6 (2022), 769.

15 Michael Haenlein and Andreas Kaplan, "A brief history of artificial intelligence: on the past, present, and future of artificial intelligence", *California Management Review* 61:4 (2019), 7.

16 Syed Mustafa Ali *et al.*, "Histories of artificial intelligence: a genealogy of power", *BJHS Themes* 8 (2023), 1–18.

17 Jonathan Penn, "Inventing intelligence: on the history of complex information processing and artificial intelligence in the United States in the mid-twentieth century" (PhD thesis, University of Cambridge, 2020), https://doi.org/10.17863/CAM.63087.

18 Jon Agar, *The Government Machine: A Revolutionary History of the Computer* (Cambridge, MA: MIT Press, 2003).

19 Gernot Grabher and Jonas König, "Disruption, embedded. A Polanyian framing of the platform economy", *Sociologica* 14:1 (2020), 95–118.

20 Revati Prasad, "People as data, data as oil: the digital sovereignty of the Indian state", *Information, Communication & Society* 25:6 (2022), 801–15; Cohen, "The biopolitical public domain".

21 Nick Couldry and Ulises A. Mejias, *The Costs of Connection: How Data Is Colonizing Human Life and Appropriating It for Capitalism* (Stanford, CA: Stanford University Press, 2019).

22 Pistor, *The Code of Capital*.

23 Kean Birch, *Data Enclaves* (Cham, CH: Palgrave Macmillan, 2023).

24 Data is not inherently useful. It requires extensive processing (cleaning, categorization, annotation and more) before it can become valuable. AI relies heavily on human effort, particularly through what has been termed "ghost work", which often exacts an enormous toll on the workers performing it. See Mary L. Gray and Siddharth Suri, *Ghost Work: How to Stop Silicon Valley from Building a New Global Underclass* (New York: Houghton Mifflin Harcourt, 2019).

25 Sarah Myers West *et al.*, *Discriminating Systems: Gender, Race, and Power in AI* (AI Now Institute, 2019).

26 Nur Ahmed *et al.*, "The growing influence of industry in AI research", *Science* 379:6635 (2023), 884–6.

27 Di Battista *et al.*, *The Future of Jobs Report 2023*.

28 Singla *et al.*, *The State of AI in Early 2024*.

29 Nicolas de Bellefonds *et al.*, *Where's the Value in AI?* (BCG, 2024); Kristina McElheran *et al.*, "AI adoption in America: who, what, and where", *Journal of Economics & Management Strategy* 33:2 (2024), 375–415.

30 George Hammond, "Big Tech outspends venture capital firms in AI investment frenzy", *Financial Times*, 29 December 2023.

31 Stephen Morris and Rafe Uddin, "Big Tech lines up over $300bn in AI spending for 2025", *Financial Times*, 7 February 2025.

32 David Cahn, "AI's $600B question", *Sequoia Capital*, 20 June 2024.

33 Tabby Kinder *et al.*, "'Godmother of AI' Fei-Fei Li builds $1bn start-up in 4 months", *Financial Times*, 17 July 2024.

34 Daub, *What Tech Calls Thinking*.

35 Peter Hall and David Soskice, *Varieties of Capitalism: The Institutional Foundations of Comparative Advantage* (Oxford: Oxford University Press, 2001).

36 Fernando van der Vlist *et al.*, "Big AI: cloud infrastructure dependence and the industrialisation of artificial intelligence", *Big Data & Society* 11:1 (2024).

37 Alan Dignam, "Artificial intelligence, tech corporate governance and the public interest regulatory response", *Cambridge Journal of Regions, Economy and Society* 13:1 (2020), 37–54.

38 Jai Vipra and Sarah Myers West, "Computational power and AI", AI Now Institute, 27 September 2023, https://ainowinstitute.org/publications/compute-and-ai: last accessed 9 September 2025.

39 Maslej *et al.*, *Artificial Intelligence Index Report 2024*, 156.

40 Mitchell, *Artificial Intelligence*.

41 Pablo Villalobos *et al.*, "Will we run out of data? Limits of LLM scaling based on human-generated data", preprint, 4 June 2024, http://arxiv.org/abs/2211.04325.

42 Cade Metz *et al.*, "How tech giants cut corners to harvest data for A.I.", *The New York Times*, 8 April 2024.

43 Jack Clark, "Import AI 310: AlphaZero learned chess like humans learn chess; capability emergence in language models; Demoscene AI", 28 November 2022, https://jack-clark.net/2022/11/28/import-ai-310-alphazero-learned-chess-like-humans-learn-chess-capability-emergence-in-language-models-demoscene-ai/: last accessed 9 September 2025.

44 Kai-Fu Lee, *AI Superpowers: China, Silicon Valley, and the New World Order* (New York: Houghton Mifflin, 2018).

45 Jeffrey Ding, "The diffusion deficit in scientific and technological power: re-assessing China's rise", *Review of International Political Economy* 31:1 (2024), 173–98.

46 Crawford, *Atlas of AI*.

47 Camilla Hodgson and Stephen Morris, "Google emissions jump nearly 50% over five years as AI use surges", *Financial Times*, 2 July 2024.

48 Pranshu Verma and Shelly Tan, "A bottle of water per email: the hidden environmental costs of using AI chatbots", *The Washington Post*, 18 September 2024.

49 Bender *et al.*, "On the dangers of stochastic parrots".

Chapter 3: American AI and the Chinese challenge

1 Michael G. Jacobides *et al.*, "The evolutionary dynamics of the artificial intelligence ecosystem", *Strategy Science* 6:4 (2021), 412–35.

2 David Meyer, "The cost of training AI could soon become too much to bear", *Fortune*, 4 April 2024.

3 Sida Peng *et al.*, "The impact of AI on developer productivity: evidence from GitHub Copilot", preprint, 2023, www.arxiv.org/abs/2302.06590.

4 Ben Cottier *et al.*, "The rising costs of training frontier AI models", preprint, 2024, www.arxiv.org/abs/2405.21015.

5 Paul Scharre, *Future-Proofing Frontier AI Regulation: Projecting Future Compute for Frontier AI Models* (CNAS, 2024), 25.

6 Sarah Burkhardt and Bernhard Rieder, "Foundation models are platform models: prompting and the political economy of AI", *Big Data & Society* 11:2 (2024).

7   Nick Srnicek, *Platform Capitalism* (Cambridge: Polity, 2017).
8   Nick Srnicek, "Data, compute, labor", in Mark Graham and Fabian Ferrari (eds), *Digital Work in the Planetary Market* (Cambridge, MA: MIT Press, 2022).
9   van der Vlist *et al.*, "Big AI", 6.
10 Tobias J. Klinge *et al.*, "Augmenting digital monopolies: a corporate financialization perspective on the rise of Big Tech", *Competition & Change* 27:2 (2023), 332–53.
11 van der Vlist *et al.*, "Big AI", 5.
12 Théophane Hartmann, "French MPs voice sovereignty, competition concerns after Microsoft-Mistral AI deal", *Euractiv*, 28 February 2024.
13 Amba Kak *et al.*, "Make no mistake – AI is owned by Big Tech", *MIT Technology Review*, 5 December 2023.
14 Maslej *et al.*, *Artificial Intelligence Index Report 2024*, 56–7.
15 David Gray Widder *et al.*, "Why 'open' AI systems are actually closed, and why this matters", *Nature* 635:8040 (2024), 827–33.
16 Chris Miller, *Chip War: The Fight for the World's Most Critical Technology* (London: Simon & Schuster, 2022); Matt Sheehan, "China's AI regulations and how they get made", Carnegie Endowment for International Peace, 10 July 2023, https://carnegie-production-assets.s3.amazonaws.com/static/files/202307-Sheehan_Chinese%20AI%20gov-1.pdf: last accessed 9 September 2025.
17 Quoted in Josh Ye, "China's AI 'war of a Hundred Models' heads for a shakeout", Reuters, 21 September 2023, https://www.reuters.com/technology/chinas-ai-war-hundred-models-heads-shakeout-2023-09-21/: last accessed 9 September 2025.
18 Giorgia Sgueglia, "China robotics industry: opportunities for foreign stakeholders", China Briefing, 30 January 2025, https://www.china-briefing.com/news/china-robotics-industry-what-are-the-opportunities-for-foreign-stakeholders/: last accessed 9 September 2025.
19 See www.statista.com/statistics/1446052/worldwide-spending-on-ai-by-industry: last accessed 9 September 2025.
20 Nestor Maslej *et al.*, *Artificial Intelligence Index Report 2025* (Stanford University Institute for Human-Centered AI, 2025), 247.
21 See www.oecd.ai/en/data?selectedArea=investments-in-ai-and-data&selectedVisualization=top-ai-start-ups-per-country-and-industry: last accessed 9 September 2025.
22 Maslej *et al.*, *Artificial Intelligence Index Report 2024*, 403–4.
23 Jacob Larson *et al.*, "The evolution of artificial intelligence (AI) spending by the U.S. government", Brookings Institution, 26 March 2024, https://www.brookings.edu/articles/the-evolution-of-artificial-intelligence-ai-spending-by-the-u-s-government/: last accessed 9 September 2025.
24 See https://nsf-gov-resources.nsf.gov/2023-10/NAIRR-TF-Final-Report-2023.pdf: last accessed 9 September 2025.
25 Dignam, "Artificial intelligence, tech corporate governance and the public interest regulatory response".
26 Corporate Europe Observatory, "Lobbying power of Amazon, Google and Co. continues to grow", 2023, https://corporateeurope.org/en/2023/09/lobbying-power-amazon-google-and-co-continues-grow: last accessed 9 September 2025.
27 Bram Vranken, "Big Tech lobbying is derailing the AI Act", *Social Europe*, 24 November 2023.
28 Corporate Europe Observatory, "How Big Tech's revolving doors erode EU antitrust laws", 28 October 2024, https://corporateeurope.org/en/2024/10/how-big-techs-revolving-doors-erode-eu-antitrust-laws: last accessed 9 September 2025.
29 Hayden Field, "OpenAI expects revenue will triple to $12.7 billion this year, source says", CNBC, 26 March 2025, https://www.cnbc.com/2025/03/26/openai-expects-revenue-will-triple-to-12point7-billion-this-year-sources-say.html: last accessed 9 September 2025.

30 Daron Acemoglu, "The simple macroeconomics of AI", NBER Working Papers no. w32487 (NBER, 2024), https://www.nber.org/papers/w32487: last accessed 9 September 2025 .

31 Robert Armstrong, "It's an AI market now", *Financial Times*, 20 June 2024.

32 Richard Waters, "Nvidia tide is lifting the tech sector", *Financial Times*, 20 June 2024.

33 Armstrong, "It's an AI market now".

34 Cahn, "AI's $600B Question".

35 Stephanie Palazzolo and Erin Woo, "OpenAI's annualized revenue doubles to $3.4 billion since late 2023", *The Information*, 12 June 2024; Maria Heeter and Stephanie Palazzolo, "Anthropic projects at least $850 million in annualized revenue rate next year", *The Information*, 26 December 2023.

36 Cade Metz *et al.*, "A.I. start-ups face a rough financial reality check", *The New York Times*, 29 April 2024.

37 See www.sacra.com/c/anduril: last accessed 9 September 2025.

38 Eugene Kim, "Wall Street worries about revenue 'round-tripping,' after big AI deals by cloud giants including Amazon and Google", *Business Insider*, 22 May 2024.

39 See www.statista.com/chart/18819/worldwide-market-share-of-leading-cloud-infra structure-service-providers: last accessed 9 September 2025.

40 Kimberley Kao and Raffaele Huang, "Chips or not, Chinese AI pushes ahead", *The Wall Street Journal*, 23 August 2024.

41 Lee, *AI Superpowers*.

42 John Lee, "The rise of China's tech sector: the making of an internet empire", *The Interpreter*, 4 May 2017.

43 Maslej *et al.*, *Artificial Intelligence Index Report 2025*, 257.

44 See www.oecd.ai/en/data?selectedArea=investments-in-ai-and-data&selectedVisualization= vc-investments-in-ai-by-country: last accessed 9 September 2025.

45 See www.oecd.ai/en/data?selectedArea=investments-in-ai-and-data&selectedVisualization= total-vc-investments-in-ai-by-country-and-industry: last accessed 9 September 2025.

46 Steve Rolf and Seth Schindler, "The US–China rivalry and the emergence of state platform capitalism", *Environment and Planning A: Economy and Space* 55:5 (2023), 1261.

47 Zijing Wu and Eleanor Olcott, "Huawei delivers advanced AI chip 'Cluster' to Chinese clients cut off from Nvidia", *Financial Times*, 30 April 2025.

48 Stefan Schmalz, "Varieties of digital capitalism and the US–China rivalry: the rise of com-peting technological spheres", *Critical Sociology*, 51:4–5, 867–6 (2025), 871.

49 Willem H. Gravett, "Digital Coloniser? China and artificial intelligence in Africa", *Survival. Global Politics and Strategy* 62:2 (2020), 153–78.

50 Feldstein, "The road to digital unfreedom", 48f.

51 See www.oecd.ai/en/data?selectedArea=investments-in-ai-and-data&selectedVisualization= vc-investments-in-ai-by-country: last accessed 9 September 2025.

52 See www.pwc.com/sg/en/publications/assets/rise-of-china-silicon-dragon.pdf: last accessed 9 September 2025.

53 Crunchbase News, "US-educated founders, born in Asia, find it advantageous for their startups to grow at home", 27 August 2017, https://news.crunchbase.com/startups/us-educated-founders-born-asia-find-advantageous-startups-grow-home/: last accessed 9 September 2025.

54 John Lee, "The rise of China's tech sector: the digital Great Game", *The Interpreter*, 5 May 2017.

55 Neil Savage, "The race to the top among the world's leaders in artificial intelligence", *Nature* 588:7837 (2020), S102–4.

56 Kai Jia and Martin Kenney, "The Chinese platform business group: an alternative to the Silicon Valley model?", *Journal of Chinese Governance* 7:1 (2022), 58–80.

57 Jing Cheng and Jinghan Zeng, "Shaping AI's future? China in global AI governance", *Journal of Contemporary China* 32:143 (2023), 800.
58 Angela Huyue Zhang, "The promise and perils of China's regulation of artificial intelligence", *Columbia Journal of Transnational Law* 63:1 (2025).
59 Frank Zhao and Jesse Heatley, "China's master plan for IT dominance", *The Diplomat*, 11 August 2016.
60 Zhang, "The promise and perils of China's regulation of artificial intelligence".
61 Lu and Qiu, "Empowerment or warfare?", 780.
62 Martin Beraja et al., *Exporting the Surveillance State via Trade in AI*, no. w31676 (NBER, 2023).
63 Bibo Lin, "Beyond authoritarianism and liberal democracy: understanding China's artificial intelligence impact in Africa", *Information, Communication & Society* 27:6 (2024), 1127.
64 Helen Warrell et al., "Exporting Chinese surveillance: the security risks of 'smart cities'", *Financial Times*, 9 June 2021.
65 Josh Ye, "Baidu says AI chatbot 'Ernie Bot' has attracted 200 million users", *Reuters*, 16 April 2024.
66 Jeffrey Ding, *Technology and the Rise of Great Powers: How Diffusion Shapes Economic Competition* (Princeton, NJ: Princeton University Press, 2024).
67 Ding, "The diffusion deficit in scientific and technological power", 189.
68 Lee, *AI Superpowers*.
69 The Economist, "China and America are racing to develop the best AI. But who is ahead in using it?", 3 April 2025, https://www.economist.com/business/2025/04/03/china-and-america-are-racing-to-develop-the-best-ai-but-who-is-ahead-in-using-it: last accessed 9 September 2025.

Chapter 4: Uneven effects across and within sectors

1 Butollo, "Digitalization and the geographies of production"; Martin Kenney and John Zysman, "The platform economy: restructuring the space of capitalist accumulation", *Cambridge Journal of Regions, Economy and Society* 13:1 (2020), 55–76.
2 Peter Dauvergne, *AI in the Wild: Sustainability in the Age of Artificial Intelligence* (Cambridge, MA: MIT Press, 2020).
3 Shannon Vallor, *The AI Mirror: How to Reclaim Our Humanity in an Age of Machine Thinking* (Oxford: Oxford University Press, 2024).
4 Acemoglu, "The simple macroeconomics of AI".
5 Robert Armstrong and Aiden Reiter, "Anatomy of a rout", *Financial Times*, 6 August 2024.
6 Birch, *Data Enclaves*.
7 Brett Christophers, "Making finance productive", *Economy and Society* 40:1 (2011), 112–40.
8 Singla et al., *The State of AI in Early 2024*.
9 de Bellefonds et al., *Where's the Value in AI?*; McElheran et al., "AI adoption in America".
10 Maslej et al., *Artificial Intelligence Index Report 2024*, 242.
11 Singla et al., *The State of AI in Early 2024*.
12 *Ibid.*
13 de Bellefonds et al., *Where's the Value in AI?*
14 Joseph Briggs and Devesh Kodnani, *The Potentially Large Effects of Artificial Intelligence on Economic Growth* (Goldman Sachs, 2023).
15 Dauvergne, *AI in the Wild*.

16 Bernard Marr, "The incredible ways John Deere is using artificial intelligence to transform farming", *Forbes*, 9 March 2018, https://www.forbes.com/sites/bernardmarr/2018/03/09/the-incredible-ways-john-deere-is-using-artificial-intelligence-to-transform-farming/: last accessed 9 September 2025.

17 Emily Olsen, "HHS lays out strategic plan for healthcare AI", *Healthcare Dive*, 14 January 2025, https://www.healthcaredive.com/news/hhs-healthcare-ai-strategic-plan/737207/: last accessed 9 September 2025.

18 See https://u.ae/en/about-the-uae/strategies-initiatives-and-awards/strategies-plans-and-visions/government-services-and-digital-transformation/uae-strategy-for-artificial-intelligence: last accessed 9 September 2025.

19 See www.ecologie.gouv.fr/sites/default/files/documents/dgitm-strategie-vehicule-automatise-et-connectee-2022-2025-EN-short-V2_0.pdf: last accessed 9 September 2025.

20 Beraja *et al.*, *Exporting the Surveillance State via Trade in AI*.

21 Regine Paul, "Can critical policy studies outsmart AI? Research agenda on artificial intelligence technologies and public policy", *Critical Policy Studies* 16:4 (2022), 497. See section IV in Regine Paul *et al.* (eds), *Handbook on Public Policy and Artificial Intelligence* (Cheltenham: Elgar, 2024).

22 European Commission, *White Paper on Artificial Intelligence: A European Approach to Excellence and Trust* (2020), https://commission.europa.eu/system/files/2020-02/commission-white-paper-artificial-intelligence-feb2020_en.pdf: last accessed 9 September 2025.

23 Paul *et al.*, *Handbook on Public Policy and Artificial Intelligence*.

24 Pablo Fuentes Nettel *et al.*, *Government AI Readiness Index 2024* (Oxford Insights, 2024).

25 Mavis Machirori, *Spending Wisely: Redesigning the Landscape for the Procurement of AI in Local Government* (Ada Lovelace Institute, 2024).

26 Pasquinelli, *The Eye of the Master*.

27 Kathryn Bonney *et al.*, *Tracking Firm Use of AI in Real Time: A Snapshot from the Business Trends and Outlook Survey*, no. w32319 (NBER, 2024).

28 See www.ec.europa.eu/eurostat/statistics-explained/index.php?title=Use_of_artificial_intelligence_in_enterprises: last accessed 9 September 2025; Kai Shen *et al.*, *The Next Frontier for AI in China Could Add $600 Billion to Its Economy* (McKinsey, 2022).

29 Flavio Calvino and Luca Fontanelli, "A portrait of AI adopters across countries: firm characteristics, assets' complementarities and productivity", OECD Science, Technology and Industry Working Papers no. 2023/02 (2023).

30 Singla *et al.*, *The State of AI in Early 2024*.

31 Heidi Heimberger *et al.*, "Exploring the factors driving AI adoption in production: a systematic literature review and future research agenda", *Information Technology and Management*, ahead of print, 23 August 2024.

32 See www.oecd.ai/en/data?selectedArea=investments-in-ai-and-data&selectedVisualization=total-vc-investments-in-ai-by-country-and-industry: last accessed 9 September 2025.

33 Anjana J. Atapattu *et al.*, "Challenges in achieving artificial intelligence in agriculture", in Siddharth Singh Chouhan *et al.* (eds), *Artificial Intelligence Techniques in Smart Agriculture* (Cham, CH: Springer, 2024).

34 Sören Pinkow, "Digital farm: farmers expect use of artificial intelligence to triple", *Continental AG*, 18 March 2024, https://www.continental.com/en/press/press-releases/20240318-agriculture-transition/: last accessed 9 September 2025.

35 Alesia Khlusevich *et al.*, "Artificial intelligence and hospitality: a challenging relationship", in Katerina Berezina *et al.* (eds), *Information and Communication Technologies in Tourism 2024* (Cham, CH: Springer, 2024).

36 Srnicek, *Platform Capitalism*.

37 Thomas Kurian, "How SunPower is using Google Cloud to create a sustainable busi-ness", Google Cloud Blog, 11 May 2019, https://cloud.google.com/blog/topics/customers/how-sunpower-is-using-google-cloud-to-create-a-sustainable-business: last accessed 9 September 2025.

38 Silvia Weko, *Phasing-out Big Oil, Phasing-in Big Tech? The Importance of Data and AI for the Energy Transition* (University of Sussex, 2024).

39 Kana Inagaki and David Keohane, "Japan's copyright rules draw AI groups – and alarm from creators", *Financial Times*, 22 July 2024.

40 Tripp Mickle, "The A.I. boom has an unlikely early winner: wonky consultants", *The New York Times*, 26 June 2024.

41 See www.statista.com/chart/18819/worldwide-market-share-of-leading-cloud-infra structure-service-providers: last accessed 9 September 2025.

42 Maarten Kuil *et al.*, *European IaaS/PaaS Market* (BDO, 2024).

43 Cédric Durand, *How Silicon Valley Unleashed Techno-Feudalism* (London: Verso, 2024); See also Vali Stan, "Big Tech rentiership and the techno-feudal hypothesis", *The New School Economic Review* 13 (April 2025), 13–28.

44 Herman Mark Schwartz, "Global secular stagnation and the rise of intellectual prop-erty monopoly", *Review of International Political Economy* 29:5 (2022), 1448–76; Cecilia Rikap, "Intellectual monopolies as a new pattern of innovation and technological regime", *Industrial and Corporate Change* 33:5 (2024), 1037–62.

45 Tara Balakrishnan *et al.*, *The State of AI in 2020* (McKinsey, 2020).

46 de Bellefonds *et al.*, *Where's the Value in AI?*

47 *Ibid.*

48 Aimilia Protogerou *et al.*, "Determinants of young firms' innovative performance: empir-ical evidence from Europe", *Research Policy* 46:7 (2017), 1312–26.

49 Schwartz, "Global secular stagnation and the rise of intellectual property monopoly".

50 Bonney *et al.*, *Tracking Firm Use of AI in Real Time*; Calvino and Fontanelli, "A portrait of AI adopters across countries".

51 Tim O'Reilly *et al.*, "Algorithmic attention rents: a theory of digital platform market power", *Data & Policy* 6 (2024).

52 Singla *et al.*, *The State of AI in Early 2024*.

53 Pascale Davies, "Why OpenAI's voice mode, Meta, and Apple's AI aren't in Europe yet", *Euronews*, 10 August 2024.

54 Samuele Fratini *et al.*, "Digital sovereignty: a descriptive analysis and a critical evaluation of existing models", *Digital Society* 3:3 (2024), 59.

Chapter 5: Uneven effects on labour

1 Judy Wajcman, *Pressed for Time. The Acceleration of Life in Digital Capitalism* (Chicago, IL: University of Chicago Press, 2015).

2 Aaron Bastani, *Fully Automated Luxury Communism* (London: Verso, 2019).

3 David Spencer *et al.*, *Digital Automation and the Future of Work* (EPRS, 2021), 16f.

4 Carl Benedikt Frey and Michael Osborne, *The Future of Employment: How Susceptible Are Jobs to Computerisation?* (Oxford Martin School, 2013).

5 Melanie Arntz *et al.*, "Revisiting the risk of automation", *Economics Letters* 159:C (2017), 157–60; Ljubica Nedelkoska and Glenda Quintini, "Automation, skills use and training", no. 202, OECD Social, Employment and Migration Working Papers (OECD Publishing, 2018), https://doi.org/10.1787/2e2f4eea-en: last accessed 9 September 2025.

6   Attilio Di Battista *et al.*, *The Future of Jobs Report 2025* (WEF, 2025).
7   Carl Benedikt Frey, *The Technology Trap: Capital, Labor, and Power in the Age of Automation* (Princeton, NJ: Princeton University Press, 2019).
8   Frey and Osborne, *The Future of Employment*.
9   *Ibid.*, 45.
10 Thomas Piketty, *Capital in the Twenty-First Century* (Cambridge, MA: Harvard University Press, 2014).
11 Di Battista *et al.*, *The Future of Jobs Report 2025*, 23.
12 Erik Brynjolfsson *et al.*, "Generative AI at work", no. w31161 (NBER, 2023).
13 Peng *et al.*, "The impact of AI on developer productivity".
14 Xiang Hui *et al.*, "The short-term effects of generative artificial intelligence on employment: evidence from an online labor market", *Organization Science* 35:6 (2024), 1977–89.
15 Carlo Pizzinelli *et al.*, "Labor market exposure to AI: cross-country differences and distributional implications", IMF Working Papers 2023, no. 216 (2023).
16 Nathan Wilmers, "Generative AI and the future of inequality", *An MIT Exploration of Generative AI*, March 2024, https://doi.org/10.21428/e4baedd9.777b7123: last accessed 9 September 2025.
17 William Crofton and Stephanie Stacey, "Draw your own chart game: how well do you know the jobs market?", *Financial Times*, 19 December 2024.
18 Di Battista *et al.*, *The Future of Jobs Report 2025*.
19 *Ibid.*, 51.
20 AnnaLee Saxenian, *Regional Advantage: Culture and Competition in Silicon Valley and Route 128* (Cambridge, MA: Harvard University Press, 1996).
21 Daub, *What Tech Calls Thinking*.
22 Gray and Suri, *Ghost Work*.
23 Billy Perrigo, "Exclusive: the $2 per hour workers who made ChatGPT safer", *Time*, 18 January 2023.
24 Roy Heidelberg, "What's old is new: AI and bureaucracy", in Paul *et al.* (eds), *Handbook of Public Policy and Artificial Intelligence*.
25 Brian Merchant, "The AI jobs crisis is here, now", *Blood in the Machine*, 27 March 2025.
26 Allison Pugh, *The Last Human Job: The Work of Connecting in a Disconnected World* (Princeton, NJ: Princeton University Press, 2024).
27 Samer Faraj *et al.*, "Working and organizing in the age of the learning algorithm", *Information and Organization* 28:1 (2018), 62–70.
28 Karl Polanyi, *The Great Transformation: The Political and Economic Origins of Our Time* (Boston, MA: Beacon Press, 2001), 39.
29 Grabher and König, "Disruption, embedded".
30 Viola Zhou and Caiwei Chen, "China's AI boom depends on an army of exploited student interns", *Rest of World*, 14 September 2023; Karen Hao and Andrea Paola Hernández, "How the AI industry profits from catastrophe", *MIT Technology Review*, 20 April 2022.
31 Clément Le Ludec *et al.*, "The problem with annotation: human labour and outsourcing between France and Madagascar", *Big Data & Society* 10:2 (2023), 9.
32 Zhuofan Li, "When being a data annotator was not yet a job: the laboratory origins of dispersible labor in computer vision research", *Socius* 10 (December 2024).
33 Joel Mokyr *et al.*, "The history of technological anxiety and the future of economic growth: is this time different?", *Journal of Economic Perspectives* 29:3 (2015), 31–50.
34 Gavin Mueller, *Breaking Things at Work: The Luddites Are Right About Why You Hate Your Job* (London: Verso, 2021); Acemoglu and Johnson, *Power and Progress*.
35 Susan Fleck *et al.*, "The compensation-productivity gap: a visual essay", *Monthly Labor Review*, January (2011), 57–69.

36 Piketty, *Capital in the Twenty-First Century*.

37 Charles Umney *et al.*, "Platform labour unrest in a global perspective: how, where and why do platform workers protest?", *Work, Employment and Society* 38:1 (2024), 3–26.

38 Mohammad Amir Anwar and Mark Graham, "Hidden transcripts of the gig economy: labour agency and the new art of resistance among African gig workers", *Environment and Planning A: Economy and Space* 52:7 (2020), 1269–91.

39 Daron Acemoglu and Pascual Restrepo, "The wrong kind of AI? Artificial intelligence and the future of labour demand", *Cambridge Journal of Regions, Economy and Society* 13:1 (2020), 25–35.

40 P. K. Agarwal, "Public administration challenges in the world of AI and bots", *Public Administration Review* 78:6 (2018), 917.

41 Christopher Hood, "A public management for all seasons?", *Public Administration* 69:1 (1991), 3–19.

42 Lina Dencik and Anne Kaun, "Datafication and the welfare state", *Global Perspectives* 1:1 (2020), 5.

43 Lyndal Sleep and Joanna Redden, "Reimagining failed automation: from neoliberal punitive automated welfare towards a politics of care", in Paul *et al.* (eds), *Handbook of Public Policy and Artificial Intelligence*.

44 Aaron Rieke *et al.*, *Essential Work: Analyzing the Hiring Technologies of Large Hourly Employers* (Los Angeles, CA: Upturn, 2021).

45 Claire Taylor and Tony Dobbins, "Social media: a (new) contested terrain between sousveillance and surveillance in the digital workplace", *New Technology, Work and Employment* 36:3 (2021), 263–84.

46 Feldstein, "The road to digital unfreedom", 42.

47 Larry Liu and Han Zhang, "Robots and protest: does increased protest among Chinese workers result in more automation?", *Socio-Economic Review* 21:3 (2023), 1751–72.

48 The archetypal example are Amazon warehouses. See Alessandro Delfanti, *The Warehouse: Workers and Robots at Amazon* (London: Pluto, 2021).

49 Johnny Ryan, "Enforcing data protection law and a whole-of-commission approach to avert the digital crisis", in Gerard Rinse Oosterwijk *et al.* (eds), *Time to Build a European Digital Ecosystem* (Friedrich-Ebert-Stiftung and FEPS, 2024).

50 Antonio Aloisi and Valerio De Stefano, *Your Boss Is an Algorithm* (London: Hart Publishing, 2022), 156; Hao and Hernández, "How the AI industry profits from catastrophe".

51 Mark Graham *et al.*, *The Risks and Rewards of Online Gig Work at the Global Margins* (Oxford Internet Institute, 2017).

52 Li, "When being a data annotator was not yet a job", 2.

53 *Ibid.*, 10f.

54 Juliet B Schor *et al.*, "Consent and contestation: how platform workers reckon with the risks of gig labor", *Work, Employment and Society* 38:5 (2024), 1423–44.

55 Hao and Hernández, "How the AI industry profits from catastrophe"; Alex J. Wood *et al.*, "Good gig, bad gig: autonomy and algorithmic control in the global gig economy", *Work, Employment and Society* 33:1 (2019), 56–75.

56 Aloisi and De Stefano, *Your Boss Is an Algorithm*, 90ff.

Chapter 6: Uneven effects in the rest of the world

1 Nettel *et al.*, *Government AI Readiness Index 2024*.

2 Meredith Whittaker, "The steep cost of capture", *Interactions* 28:6 (2021), 52.

3   Michael Kwet, "Digital colonialism: US empire and the new imperialism in the Global South", *Race & Class* 60:4 (2019), 14.

4   Adams, *The New Empire of AI*, 31.

5   Bhaskar Chakravorti *et al.*, "Charting the emerging geography of AI", *Harvard Business Review*, 12 December 2023.

6   European Commission, *White Paper on Artificial Intelligence*, 5, 12.

7   European Commission, *Communication on Artificial Intelligence for Europe* (2018), 5, https://eur-lex.europa.eu/legal-content/EN/TXT/?uri=celex:52018DC0237: last accessed 9 September 2025.

8   European Commission, "EU launches InvestAI initiative to mobilise €200 billion", 11 February 2025, www.ec.europa.eu/commission/presscorner/detail/en/ip_25_467: last accessed 9 September 2025.

9   Matt Davies, "A lost decade? The UK's industrial approach to AI", AI Now Institute, 12 March 2024.

10   Office for AI, *National AI Strategy* (London, 2021).

11   Matt Clifford, *AI Opportunities Action Plan* (DSIT, 2025).

12   Jyoti Panday and Mila T. Samtub, "Promises and pitfalls of India's AI industrial policy", *AI Now Institute*, 12 March 2024.

13   Islam Al Khatib, "Beyond techwashing: the UAE's AI industrial policy as a security regime", *AI Now Institute*, 12 March 2024.

14   Panday and Samtub, "Promises and pitfalls of India's AI industrial policy".

15   Saxenian, *The New Argonauts*.

16   Daniel Mügge, "Regulatory interdependence in AI", in Paul *et al.* (eds), *Handbook on Public Policy and Artificial Intelligence*.

17   Sabine Mokry and Julia Gurol, "Competing ambitions regarding the global governance of artificial intelligence: China, the US, and the EU", *Global Policy* 15:5 (2024), 964.

18   See www.oecd.ai/en/dashboards/overview: last accessed 10 April 2025.

19   Lee, "The rise of China's tech sector", 5 May 2017.

20   Mie Hoejris Dahl, "The Belt and Road isn't dead. It's evolving", *Foreign Policy*, 26 November 2024.

21   Vicki L. Birchfield, "From roadmap to regulation: will there be a transatlantic approach to governing artificial intelligence?", *Journal of European Integration* 46:7 (2024), 1066f.

22   For full interview data, see Paul, "European AI 'trusted throughout the world' ", 1074.

23   Niall Duggan, "China – the champion of the developing world: a study of China's new development model and its role in changing global economic governance", *Politics & Policy* 48:5 (2020), 836–58.

24   Xinhua, "At G20 Summit, Xi urges a fair, equitable global governance system", 19 November 2024, https://english.news.cn/20241119/9a1789ff8653491a80a9879008f9dc65/c.html: last accessed 9 September 2025.

25   See www.cac.gov.cn/2023-10/18/c_1699291032884978.htm: last accessed 9 September 2025.

26   Jinping Xi, "Keynote Speech at Opening Ceremony of Third Belt and Road Forum for International Cooperation", China News Service, 18 October 2023.

27   *Ibid.*

28   Lu and Qiu, "Empowerment or warfare?", 776.

29   Dahl, "The Belt and Road isn't dead".

30   Richard Heeks *et al.*, "China's digital expansion in the Global South: systematic literature review and future research agenda", *The Information Society* 40:2 (2024), 83.

31   Bill Drexel and Hannah Kelley, "Behind China's plans to build AI for the world", *Politico*, 30 November 2023, https://www.politico.com/news/magazine/2023/11/30/china-global-ai-plans-00129160: last accessed 9 September 2025.

32   Schmalz, "Varieties of digital capitalism and the US–China rivalry", 2.

33   Vincent Brussee, "China's social credit score – untangling myth from reality", *MERICS*, 11 February 2022.

34   Ursula von der Leyen, "Speech by President von Der Leyen at the Artificial Intelligence Action Summit", European Commission, 11 February 2025, www.ec.europa.eu/commission/presscorner/api/files/document/print/en/speech_25_471/SPEECH_25_471_EN.pdf: last accessed 9 September 2025.

35   Chloe Cornish and Madhumita Murgia, "Abu Dhabi in talks to invest in OpenAI chip venture", *Financial Times*, 15 March 2024.

36   Katie McQue *et al.*, "The global struggle over how to regulate AI", *Rest of World*, 21 January 2025.

37   Adekemi Omotubora and Subhajit Basu, "Decoding and reimagining AI governance beyond colonial shadows", in Paul *et al.* (eds), *Handbook on Public Policy and Artificial Intelligence*.

38   Couldry and Mejias, *The Costs of Connection*; Kwet, "Digital colonialism".

39   Adams, *The New Empire of AI*, 70.

40   Chinasa T. Okolo, "AI in the Global South: opportunities and challenges towards more inclusive governance", Brookings Institution, 1 November 2023.

41   Guilherme Cavalcante Silva, "Articulating AI futures for Brazil: on different regimes of technological solutionism", Critical Policy Studies, 2025, 1–20.

42   Sandra Makumbirofa, "Reflections on South Africa's AI industrial policy", AI Now Institute, 12 March 2024.

43   Abeba Birhane, "Algorithmic colonization of Africa", *SCRIPT-Ed* 17:2 (2020), 392.

44   Couldry and Mejias, *The Costs of Connection*.

45   Birhane, "Algorithmic colonization of Africa".

46   Zhou and Chen, "China's AI boom depends on an army of exploited student interns".

47   Milagros Miceli *et al.*, *Who Trains the Data for European Artificial Intelligence?*, Report of the European Microworkers Communication and Outreach Initiative (EnCOre, 2023–2024) (DAIR Institute, Weizenbaum Institute and DiPLab, 2024).

48   *Training AI Takes Heavy Toll on Kenyans Working for $2 an Hour*, 60 Minutes, 2024, www.youtube.com/watch?v=qZS50KXjAX0: last accessed 9 September 2025.

49   See Hao and Hernández, "How the AI industry profits from catastrophe" for similar reports on Scale AI operating in Venezuela".

50   Seyram Avle, "Hardware and data in the platform era: Chinese smartphones in Africa", *Media, Culture & Society* 44:8 (2022), 1474.

51   Lin, "Beyond authoritarianism and liberal democracy", 1135.

52   Couldry and Mejias, *The Costs of Connection*; Zuboff, *The Age of Surveillance Capitalism*.

53   Kwet, "Digital colonialism", 7f.

54   Heather A. Horst *et al.*, "Beyond extraction: data strategies from the Global South", *New Media & Society* 26:3 (2024), 1366.

55   Avle, "Hardware and data in the platform era", 1483.

56   Gravett, "Digital coloniser?", 155f.

57   Lin, "Beyond authoritarianism and liberal democracy", 1135.

58   Adams, *The New Empire of AI*, 37.

59   Simon Michael Taylor *et al.*, "Artificial intelligence from colonial India: race, statistics, and facial recognition in the Global South", *Science, Technology, & Human Values* 48:3 (2023), 671. We owe insights about this fascinating statistical method and its mutation to a global FRT standard to the authors.

60   Payal Arora, *From Pessimism to Promise: Lessons from the Global South on Designing Inclusive Tech* (Cambridge, MA: MIT Press, 2024).

61 Adams, *The New Empire of AI*, 74.
62 See www.deeplearningindaba.com/about/our-mission: last accessed 9 September 2025.
63 Disrupt Africa, "The African Tech Startups Funding Report 2024", 2025, www. disruptafrica.com/wp-content/uploads/2025/03/The-African-Tech-Startups-Funding-Report-2024.pdf.
64 AU–EU Digital Economy Task Force, *New Africa-Europe Digital Economy Partnership: Accelerating the Achievement of the Sustainable Development Goals* (2021), 41, https:// international-partnerships.ec.europa.eu/system/files/2021-01/new-africa-eu-digital-economy_en_0.pdf: last accessed 9 September 2025.
65 Tage Kene-Okafor, "African fintech Flutterwave triples valuation to over \$3B after \$250M Series D", *TechCrunch*, 16 February 2022.
66 *The Economist*, What Happened to the Artificial-Intelligence Revolution?, 2 July 2024, https://www.economist.com/finance-and-economics/2024/07/02/what-happened-to-the-artificial-intelligence-revolution: last accessed 9 September 2025.
67 McQue *et al.*, "The global struggle over how to regulate AI".
68 See www.ghananlp.org: last accessed 9 September 2025.

Chapter 7: AI futures reconsidered

1 Adams, *The New Empire of AI*, 54.
2 Marietje Schaake, *The Tech Coup: How to Save Democracy from Silicon Valley* (Princeton, NJ: Princeton University Press, 2024).
3 Johan Söderberg, *Hacking Capitalism: The Free and Open Source Software Movement* (Abingdon: Routledge, 2016).
4 Maslej *et al.*, Artificial Intelligence Index Report 2024, 56–7.
5 Xiaoqi Jiao *et al.*, "TinyBERT: distilling BERT for natural language understanding", pre-print, 15 October 2020, http://arxiv.org/abs/1909.10351.
6 Tom Dotan and Deepa Seetharaman, "For AI giants, smaller is sometimes better", *The Wall Street Journal*, 6 July 2024.
7 Ananya Bhattacharya, "Non-Western founders say DeepSeek is proof that innovation need not cost billions of dollars", *Rest of World*, 30 January 2025.
8 Geming Xia *et al.*, "Poisoning attacks in federated learning: a survey", *IEEE Access* 11 (2023), 10708–22.
9 Daniel Curto-Millet and Alberto Corsín Jiménez, "The sustainability of open source commons", *European Journal of Information Systems* 32:5 (2023), 763–81.
10 Widder *et al.*, "Why 'open' AI systems are actually closed".
11 See www.imda.gov.sg/resources/press-releases-factsheets-and-speeches/press-releases/2023/sg-to-develop-southeast-asias-first-llm-ecosystem: last accessed 9 September 2025.
12 Nicholas Yong, "Writers and publishers in Singapore reject a government plan to train AI on their work", *Rest of World*, 8 May 2024.
13 See www.microsoft.com/en/customers/story/18916-amref-health-africa-azure: last accessed 9 September 2025.
14 See www.indigenous-ai.net: last accessed 9 September 2025.
15 Damilare Dosumnu, "Nigerians are building affordable alternatives to AWS and Google Cloud", *Rest of World*, 25 February 2025.
16 See www.deutschlandfunk.de/schleswig-holsteins-landesregierung-wirbt-fuer-abschaffung-von-microsoft-programmen-100.html: last accessed 9 September 2025.

17 See https://openresearch.amsterdam/nl/page/121460/streven-naar-digitale-autonomie-in-amsterdam: last accessed 9 September 2025.
18 Mueller, *Breaking Things at Work*, 13.
19 Perrigo, "The $2 per hour workers who made ChatGPT safer".
20 See www.amazonlaborunion.org: last accessed 9 September 2025.
21 Mueller, *Breaking Things at Work*, 71.
22 For example, the British Trade Union Congress: Ryan Morrison, "TUC says AI puts workers at risk without legislation", *Tech Monitor*, 19 April 2023.
23 Atahualpa Blanchet, "Trade union strategies on artificial intelligence and collective bargaining on algorithms", *Equal Times*, 4 July 2024.
24 Karen Hao and Nadine Freischlad, "The gig workers fighting back against the algorithms", *MIT Technology Review*, 21 April 2022.
25 See www.cut.org.br/noticias/uso-da-inteligencia-artificial-no-trabalho-deve-ser-incluido-na-negociacao-colet-2b4a: last accessed 9 September 2025.
26 Oscar Molina *et al.*, "It takes two to code: a comparative analysis of collective bargaining and artificial intelligence", *Transfer* 29:1 (2023), 87–104.
27 Peck and Phillips, "The platform conjuncture", 93.
28 Kim Stanley Robinson, *The Ministry for the Future* (London: Orbit, 2020).

Index

accelerationism 122
agentic AI 18, 79
AI adoption
　agricultural sector 22, 61, 64, 108
　autocratic regimes 51, 98, 103
　creative industry 37, 57, 77
　diffusion patterns 52–3, 55–6
　energy sector 61, 65, 70
　financial sector 63–4
　healthcare sector 48, 61, 64
　ICT sector 63, 64
　manufacturing sector 21–2, 63–4
　public sector 52, 62, 82, 87–8, 91
　shallow vs. deep 60
AI bubble 45, 126
AI governance
　BRICS 104–5
　Chinese 7, 61, 100–3
　European 7, 23, 61, 89, 92, 100–1, 104–5
　international 100–1, 105–6
　transatlantic 103–5
　political oversight 30–3
　US 7, 100–5
AI narratives
　and labour market transformation 82–8
　and public sector management 25, 88
　optimistic 2, 58
　performativity of 8–10, 44, 58, 59
　pessimistic 3–4, 58
AI race 11–12, 47–53, 96–9, 127
AI sensitivity of economic sectors 55, 61
AI stack 35–6, 42–7

AI, definition of 18–24
AI, history of development 24–30
Alibaba 41, 49–52
algorithmic worker management 89–94
alienation (from work relations) 87–9
Alphabet 9, 34, 37–40, 44–5, 65–6, 115
　Google 5–6, 32, 44, 63, 69–70
AlphaGo 19
Altman, Sam 38–9
Amazon 20, 37, 39–40, 58, 68
　Labor Union 122
　Mechanical Turk 92
　Web Services (AWS) 20, 115, 121
Andreessen, Marc 1–2
Anthropic 40, 44–6, 71
antitrust policy 39–40, 47, 51, 69–71, 92
Apple 40, 44, 118
ASML 41, 47, 49
autocratic governance 29, 98–9, 103–4
automated interviewing 89
autonomous vehicles 39, 42, 61, 77

Baidu 41, 48–52
behaviour prediction 20
Belt and Road Initiative 49, 101
Biden, Joe 1, 11, 47, 101, 104
biometrics 23, 31, 50, 61–2, 98, 111
Boston Dynamics 23, 29
Brazil 99, 104–5, 107, 124; see also BRICS countries
BRICS countries 101, 104–5

capitalism, crises of 9–10
ChatGPT 19, 35–41, 61, 81–90; *see also* large language models (LLMs)
China 90, 110, 111; *see also* BRICS countries
  AI governance 7, 61, 100–3
  as AI contender 11, 41, 47–53, 62, 96–9
  investment 51
  tech diplomacy 100–4; *see also* Digital Silk Road
CloudWalk Technology 51, 103
constructivism 8, 88
consultancies 2, 9, 49, 59, 65, 88
copyright, violations of 32, 115–16
corporate governance in tech firms 29

DALL-E 37, 57, 78
data annotation labour 84–5, 91–2, 109
data commodification 26–7
DataProphet 21, 112
decentralized AI 118
DeepMind 19, 98
DeepSeek 8, 11, 29, 38, 40, 44
Defense Advanced Research Project Agency (DARPA) 26
Denmark 124
Digital Silk Road 49, 51, 101–3, 110
digital sovereignty 12, 66–7, 71, 121, 125
Ding, Jeffrey 33, 52
discrimination 3, 30, 62, 89

economism 4, 57, 71, 82, 84, 87
ELIZA (chatbot) 25
environmental impact of AI 29, 33–4, 57, 120
Ethiopia 95, 101, 110–11
European Union
  AI governance 7, 23, 61, 89, 92, 100–1, 104–5
  digital sovereignty 99
  expectations on AI 2, 11–12
  investment 97
Eurostack 122
extractivism 26–7, 108–9

facial recognition technologies (FRTs) 23–4, 31, 49–51, 62, 110–11
first-mover advantage 29, 96–7
Flutterwave 112

Framework Convention on AI (Council of Europe) 105
France 40, 62, 70

Gazebo 40
GDP, AI's effects on 14, 55, 57–8
Gebru, Timnit 5–6
generative AI 21, 31–2, 35–6, 57, 78–9; *see also* large language models (LLMs)
geoeconomic context 11–12; *see also* geopolitics
geopolitics 11–12, 15, 27, 124–5
  export controls 41, 47, 49
  protectionist strategies 49, 126
Germany 42, 70, 121
GitHub 19, 36–7, 78
Gojek 123; *see also* labour mobilization

Hikvision 49
hiring, use of AI in 89
Hiroshima Principles on AI 105
Huawei 47, 49–51, 110

IBM 65
iFlytek 41
India; *see also* BRICS countries
  Aadhaar system 98, 111
  AI race 86, 97–8, 112, 126
  tech diplomacy 104–5
Indigenous AI 12; *see also* resistance
Indonesia 42, 51, 123
institutions 7–8, 82, 124
  labour market 119
  welfare state 85–6
investment 37–9, 40–3, 48–9, 51, 59, 97
Israel 86, 99

Jais 98; *see also* Saudi Arabia
job augmentation 4, 73, 75–6
job creation 78, 81, 86–7
job losses
  automation and 73–7
  estimates of 74
  public sector 88
  variation across sectors 76–8
John Deere 22, 61, 108

Kenya 14, 109, 121
Keynes, John Maynard 25, 73

labour
  commodification 83, 89, 91
  connective 83
  exploitation 81–2, 86, 108–9
  mobilization 7, 122–4
  productivity 4, 56, 73–6, 84–5, 119
  shortages 75
  wage-related impact of AI 75
labour market dualization 76–7
large language models (LLMs)
  functioning 19–21
  infrastructural requirements 29,
    36, 38
  model downsizing 117–18
  resource consumption 34, 118
Lee, Kai-Fu 33, 52
Lee, Sedol 19
lobbying 44, 51

majority world 14, 95, 96, 106–12; see also
    decolonial political economy
Manus 52
market valuation (of tech firms and
    startups) 28, 37, 44, 112
Masakhane 121
Massachusetts Institute of Technology
    (MIT) 25, 81
mergers and acquisitions (M&A)
    39, 50
Meta 9, 27–9, 37, 44, 116–17
  Facebook 27, 69, 108
  Llama 40, 117
  Metaverse 18, 27, 37
Microsoft 36, 37, 40, 44, 110
Mistral 40–1, 81
Musk, Elon 3, 5, 9, 88

National Basketball Association
    (NBA) 123
network effects 22, 38, 66, 96
neural networks 20–1, 27, 31–2
Nigeria 42, 51, 121
NoMindBhutan 111
Norway 9–10
Nvidia 18, 28, 41, 44–5, 47

OECD AI Policy Observatory 100
oligopolistic tendencies 7, 29, 46, 69, 87
  alternatives to 116–19
open source 40–1, 116–17, 120
OpenAI 28, 30, 36–8, 39, 40, 44, 45, 82,
    109, 115, 122

platforms 38, 65, 69, 91–3
Platform Work Directive (EU) 92–3
Polanyi, Karl 6, 26, 73, 83–5
political economy
  comparative 6–7, 13
  cultural 9
  decolonial 14–15, 106–12
  variegated 15
process optimization 21, 61, 78
profit-driven logic 56–8, 114–19

recommender systems 22, 68
redistributive innovation 56–9
reinforcement learning 20–3, 79
resistance 119–24
robotics 21–3, 40–1, 48, 64, 79

SAP 66
Saudi Arabia 10, 41, 99, 104; see also
    BRICS countries
scalability 22, 28–30, 115
Schumpeter, Joseph 96
science and technology studies 5, 8
securitization of AI 98, 103, 106, 126
ServiceNow 21–2, 70
Shenzhen cluster 13, 99
Silicon Savannah 109, 121
Silicon Valley 13, 81, 86–7
SiloAI 81
Singapore 86, 120
SMIC 49
SoftBank 66
software-as-a-service 69–70, 115
solidarity, erosion of 6, 93–3, 123
sousveillance 90
South Africa 21, 59, 107, 110, 121; see also
    BRICS countries
standard setting 105–6
Stargate 11, 44
startups 28, 41–2, 66, 71, 112
Sub-Saharan Africa 79

Tay (chatbot) 29
tech clusters 81, 86
tech colonialism 106–12
Tencent 41, 50
Trade and Technology Council (TTC) 100, 103–5
Transsion 24, 41, 51, 102–3, 109–10
Trump, Donald 40, 43–4, 87, 101, 104–5, 126
TSMC 35, 47
Turing, Alan 24

Uber 56–7, 92–3
unions 7, 61, 86, 122
United Arab Emirates (UAE) 41, 62, 98–101
United Kingdom 62–3, 71, 97–8

United States
    AI governance 7, 100–5
    domination 35–6, 42–4, 110
    investment 12, 25–6, 43

varieties of capitalism 28
von der Leyen, Ursula 97, 104

Walmart 60
workplace surveillance 74, 90–1, 119

Xi, Jinping 11–12, 101–2
Xiaomi 50

ZTE 110
Zuckerberg, Mark 9, 27